Living with Stories

Telling, Re-telling, and Remembering

Living with Stories

Telling, Re-telling, and Remembering

Edited by
William Schneider

With Essays by
Aron L. Crowell and Estelle Oozevaseuk
Holly Cusack-McVeigh
Sherna Berger Gluck
Lorraine McConaghy
Joanne B. Mulcahy
Kirin Narayan

Utah State University Press
Logan, Utah

Utah State University Press
Logan, Utah 84322–7800
www.usu.edu/usupress

Manufactured in the United States of America
Printed on acid-free, recycled paper
ISBN 978–0–87421–689-9 (cloth)
ISBN 978–0–87421–690-5 (e-book)

Chapter 3 was first published as Aron L. Crowell and Estelle Oozevaseuk. 2006. "The St. Lawrence Island Famine and Epidemic, 1878–1880: A Yupik Narrative in Cultural and Historical Perspective." *Arctic Anthropology* 43(1):1–19.

Library of Congress Cataloging-in-Publication Data

Living with stories : telling, re-telling, and remembering / edited by William Schneider ; with essays by Aron L. Crowell ... [et al].
　　p. cm.
　Includes index.
　ISBN 978-0-87421-689-9 (cloth : alk. paper)
　1. Storytelling. 2. Folklore–Performance. 3. Oral tradition. 4. Oral history. I. Schneider, William. II. Crowell, Aron, 1952-
　　GR72.3.L58 2008
　　907–dc22

　　　　　　　　　　　　　　2007045593

Contents

1

Introduction

William Schneider

William Schneider is curator of oral history at the
Elmer Rasmuson Library, University of Alaska
Fairbanks. A long-time member of the Oral History
Association, his interests are in the dynamics of
storytelling, how people use and construct narrative to convey meaning. His most recent book
is . . . *So They Understand: Cultural Issues in Oral History.*

When we open our ears and our minds to oral tradition and personal narratives, we add layers of meaning to the oral history
accounts we have stored on our shelves. We can ask, why was this
story told at that time? Why was it told to this person? Why does the
telling differ with audience and setting? When we are open to these
questions, we become more sensitive to implied as well as explicit
meanings, and we see how stories may indirectly convey attitudes
and beliefs. These expanded areas of contextual analysis broaden
the oral historian's work beyond the words on tape and transcript
to an exploration of how the story is used in the home, on the
street, told to a daughter, and retold over time in different ways for
different reasons.

The title of this book, *Living with Stories,* emphasizes our common
belief that to really understand a story, we need to listen to how
it is used and recognize how each new narration bears the mark
of the present and a particular reason for telling. This is not new
information to scholars of oral narrative, but our focus on retellings

provides a new and appropriate frame for asking about individual stories and how they are used over time. By exploring examples of how and when people retell their stories, it is our hope that we can (1) expand appreciation for how people create and convey meaning through stories; (2) demonstrate how context and audience play out in a variety of different case studies of retellings in different cultural settings where different values, beliefs and practices influence the story and how it is told; and (3) use our focus on retellings to explore how stories are keys to how and what we remember.

As contributors to this volume, we come from the disciplines of history, anthropology, folklore, and literature. Our examples are international in scope and diverse in content and theme. Our common ground is an interest in how people use stories over time and what prompts them to remember and retell. We hope that the examples and the accompanying conversations with commentators will stimulate you to compare and contrast different kinds of storytelling and to reflect on the role of narrative in your own life.

When we live with stories and actually think about how we use narrative, we see how accounts are a resource to talk about what we think is important; they are our way of relating experience to the present, and we recognize that stories are as much about the present as the past. Telling our stories is how we construct meaning from memory, but the process is selective and many factors influence how we tell stories and why we choose to retell certain stories. In this work we demonstrate some of the ways that people use particular stories and narrative structures. The examples and reactions of the commentators lead us beyond knowing the skeletal principles of how stories work to a discussion of actual stories working in people's lives. We want you, our readers, to live with the stories that are retold here, to hear the struggle of narrators and authors to understand, to see the transformations of text over time, and to witness the efforts to remember and retell. The discussions between the authors and their discussants enriches appreciation for the most important part of being human, the ability to relate to each other through oral narrative across cultures, generations, and diverse experiences.

The Emergence of Oral History

Oral historians who do this work come from many different disciplines, and their theoretical training is as diverse as the subfields within their disciplines. History, anthropology, and folklore are the primary, although not exclusive, training grounds for professionals

who use oral history methods. Oral history is nourished today by
all three disciplines and by the librarians and archivists who man-
age the ever expanding collections of recordings. Each discipline
has a stake in how oral sources are understood and used, but the
academic roots of oral history rest in history, and in particular in
the use of interviews as a way to elicit information about what happened in the past (Ritchie 1995:1). Therefore, we start our discussion with history but quickly see that the other disciplines have
enriched a discussion within the Oral History Association that goes
beyond any one formal discipline.

Paul Thompson makes the point that the term "oral history" is
relatively new, but the idea of learning about the past directly from
interviews and stories is quite old (Thompson 2000:26). For many
years, the only way to pass on knowledge was through individual
recollections of what happened (Henige 1982:7–22). So, why is the
formal study of "oral history" relatively new? Two historical developments seem to have diverted attention from oral sources: the
growth of written texts, particularly after the printing press made
such volumes widely accessible (Henige 1982:13). Then, after
1825, the formal training of historians was strongly influenced by
the German school and what became known as the "documentary
method" (Thompson 2000:55). For many trained historians, the
focus narrowed to what could be demonstrated through written
sources. Testing for reliability and verifiability became hallmarks
of the discipline. There was little room for oral sources, particularly if they couldn't be proven by empirical evidence. The focus
was clearly and particularly on what could be demonstrated to have
occurred. It is not surprising, then, that the criteria of verifiability
(can it be determined to be true?) and reliability (is the account
correctly retold and reported?) emerged as central concerns when
the oral history movement in the United States was formally recognized in 1948 with Alan Nevins' Oral History Project at Columbia
University (Dunaway and Baum 1996:29). The idea was to learn
information from individuals who were in a place to know and
thereby fill out the historical record. For instance, consider this
definition offered by Willa Baum back in 1982 (emphasis is hers):
"Oral History is the *tape recording* of a *knowledgeable* person, by *questions and answers*, about what he/she *did or observed* of an event or
events or way of life of historical interest. The purpose is to *preserve*
that account for users, both present but especially future users, and
make it available for use" (Baum 1983:39).

At first, the effort in American oral history research was directed at those who were in positions of power and influence, "movers and shakers," the famous. The term "elite oral history" became identified with this work. The most obvious example of this is the oral history projects associated with presidential libraries, beginning in 1961 and ongoing (Ritchie 1987:591), but see also the University of California Berkeley's Regional Oral History Office roster of interviews starting in 1954 (http://Bancroft.berkeley.edu). While part of the thinking was that the rich and powerful, the educated and influential, were the people who knew and could actually contribute to the historical record, there may also have been the practical recognition that these were the people who were in the best financial position to support research. In England, there are examples of a greater interest at this time in recording the experiences of the 'ordinary' people (Thomson 2007:51).

Ironically, public funding opportunities in the United States turned in favor of ethnic and other underrepresented groups, Native Americans, Blacks, and immigrants. There was a revised interest in the interviews that had been done during the Works Progress Administration era, particularly with former slaves (Ritchie 1987:589 and http://memory.loc.gov/ammem/snhtml/snhome.html). Other works such as *Amoskeag*, the story of a factory town in New Hampshire (Hareven 1978), and *Akenfield*, the story of an English farming community (Blythe 1969), brought public recognition to the conditions of workers. More recently, Milton Rogovin and Michael Frisch's *Portraits in Steel* (1993) depicts in oral narrative and photo images the conditions of steel workers in Buffalo, New York. Events such as World War II (Terkel 1984; Gluck 1987) and the Holocaust (Lewin 1990) and the issues faced by first generation Japanese Americans (Tamura 1993) became the subjects of interviews that helped bring public recognition in a first-person way to issues of genocide, racism, and prejudice.

When taken together, the two approaches to interviewing—top down with the movers and shakers and bottom up with the workers and common folk—represented a growing realization that a story could be told differently by people whose experiences differed or who perceived the events differently, and that by working with these different perspectives we could produce a more inclusive understanding: "a story no one person could have told" (Kline 1996:20; Thomson 2007:54).

Even before the "formal" re-recognition of the role of oral sources in historical research and before the explosion of oral history programs at universities, libraries, museums, and historical societies, anthropologists, folklorists, and some trained historians were coming face to face with people whose understanding of the past was distinctly different from their own. Genealogical accounts, myths, legends, cultural reconstructions of history, and life stories were windows into how people thought about and described their history. In Africa, the work of Jan Vansina (1965) and Ruth Finnegan (1992; 1998) brought to the attention of scholars the ways Africans expressed their understandings of the past, what they recognized as "verbal arts" (Finnegan 1992). Similarly, British colonial officers, some of whom were historians, found the study and understanding of oral sources useful as they attempted to resolve disputes and administer to the empire (Henige 1982:20).

Bridging the disciplines of anthropology and history, ethnohistorians pioneered research on the histories of nonliterate societies using all forms of documentation, including the oral record (Brown 1991; Krech 1991:349; Sturtevant 1966). Ethnohistorians fostered in-depth discussions of how cultural differences could be evaluated and appreciated in an historical perspective; hence the conclusion by Krech that the field could be called anthropological history or historical anthropology to emphasize the issues raised by research about the ways that cultural groups understood and described their history (Krech 1991:365; Brown and Vibert 2003). This research has taught us the importance of heightened sensitivity to how people conceptualize history and the ways they express these meanings. Reexamination, rehearing, and dialogue over time have become hallmarks of this research, particularly where we are working through translations (Mathews and Roulette in Brown and Vibert 2003:263–292).

Another form of historical reconstruction came from anthropologists who pioneered the life history method (Lewis 1965; Mintz 1960; Radin 1963; Rosengarten 1974; Lurie 1961; Langness and Frank 1981) as a way to document the rapid changes going on in the lives of community members. Alistair Thomson also traces the interest in life histories to a recognition of the therapeutic benefits that can come from talking about one's life (Thomson 2007:59). Within the lifetimes of their subjects these authors could see the influences of acculturative forces but also the core cultural values that persisted. Many of the early life histories brought the value of first person narrative to the attention of a scholarly audience: not just the content of what the narrators said but the ways they chose to construct and tell their life stories (Titon 1980). This in turn influenced the way authors rerepresented the accounts in writing. In fact, the term "author" came to be questioned. Terms such as "oral biography," "life histories based on oral history," "oral memoir," and "oral autobiography" are reflections of this awareness and attempt to capture the roles that narrators and their collaborators assume when they tell and write their story (Schneider 2002:114–115; Dunaway 1991:257). Of course, this reflects a growing recognition of the importance of understanding and describing the relationship between the narrator and the recorder/writer (Thomson 2007:62). All of the developments just described expanded scholars' appreciation for how the oral record could be used to understand history, both in terms of what people considered historical and the ways they construct and convey that understanding to others.

The American Oral History Association is young (forty years old in 2006), and while its roots are fully planted in how oral narrative can contribute to history (in the sense of supporting documents), the developments just described extended the discussion. The association welcomed a diverse and talented group of scholars from disciplines other than history, and their work has broadened appreciation for the ways stories are used by people to talk, not just about the past, but about their lives today. Key contributions to this discussion came from folklorists whose work has been specifically recognized by the Oral History Association. For instance, in *George Magoon and the Down East Game War*, Edward "Sandy" Ives, a folklorist by training and a pioneer in the oral history movement, demonstrates that stories about the fantastic feats of a backcountry Maine moose poacher reflect how tellers and their audiences now feel about the hunting laws that impact their lives. A stretch from the facts, George Magoon is a culture hero who represents and expresses their feelings about the game regulations that favor sport hunters over local subsistence users. Similarly, Jack Santino's study of Black railcar porters, *Miles of Smiles, Years of Struggle* (1989), introduces us to the ways that the porters use stories to describe how they overcame adversity on a daily basis and their respect for the honesty and integrity of their leader, A. Phillip Randolph. Other members of the oral history community, such as Barbara Allen (Bogart) in the stories she collected on the American West, *In Place*, lead us beyond narrative as description of events to stories as also reflections of the attitudes and sentiments of the tellers and their audiences.[1]

With this background, it is not surprising that the Oral History Association welcomed Julie Cruikshank as its keynote speaker for the 1999 meeting. Cruikshank, a Canadian anthropologist with deep roots in the Yukon, used the opportunity to retell the story of Ḵaax̱'achgóok. In her work with this story, Cruikshank traces the different occasions and ways that Tlingit and Tagish elder Angela Sidney retold the story of Ḵaax̱'achgóok. Each telling carries the story of how he was lost at sea for a time but found his way home. That's the basic story but it doesn't end there. The story takes on additional meaning each time Angela Sidney tells it: to celebrate the return of her son from WWII (like Ḵaax̱'achgóok, who was lost at sea, her son returned safely), to commemorate the opening of Yukon College (built in the home region; so young adults will not have to leave for school and be lost to the community, like Ḵaax̱'achgóok who was lost for a time at sea). Cruikshank demonstrates that this story, like all stories, isn't just about the past. Angela Sidney, through Julie Cruikshank's work, teaches us what it means to appreciate the "social life of stories" and to recognize how people can "live life like a story" (Cruikshank 1990, 1998). Each telling adds new dimensions to our understanding and interpretation. Our debt to Cruikshank is evidenced in our choice of the title for this book.

Living with Stories

In David William Cohen's *The Combing of History*, we see further evidence of how the present can expand the way we understand and retell our history. Cohen argues that in our understanding and reporting about the past, we continually add layers of meaning as new information is forthcoming and as our circumstances shed new light on old stories. In Cohen's terms, we are involved in a "production of history" based on an accumulation of influences such as audience, setting, recognition of need or interest, and the events that precede our decisions to recollect and retell. In this view, past tellings and present circumstances become part of our understanding of the story and influence how we use the story to convey meaning in the future. For Cohen and others like Trouillot (1995) and Hamilton et al. (2002), who might be loosely grouped as postmodernists, history is not just what can be shown to have occurred; it is also the record of how our understandings of the past evolve and inform us in the present. For these scholars, stories aren't bound; they grow with each new telling and opportunity to find meaning and to relate the past to the present.

Folklorist John Miles Foley makes the point that stories contain "tagged potentials": that is, by examining the texts and the way the story is constructed and with close attention to the historic context, we can discern how the story was used and its meaning (Pathways Project, Oral Traditions and the Internet, posting for Friday, April 15, 2005: "Excavating an Epic"). On the surface, tagged potentials seem similar to the production of history, the chance to see how a story could be used in new and different contexts. Both Cohen and Foley are grappling with the multitude of ways we draw meaning from stories and the illusiveness of trying to confer meaning to a singular interpretation from one point in time. For Foley, the challenge is how to represent and preserve the fluidity of ancient texts, to determine the range of intended meaning and use. He sees clues in the way the texts are structured and the ways words were used in their historic context. For Foley, with adequate attention to the historic context and the performance today, we can discern the range and meaning of the stories.

However, the application of "tagged potentials" to the modern setting is problematic. It is clear that we interpret ancient texts and apply them to our lives (Schneider 2003), but in the process we also create new "tagged potentials." We may use terms or sayings from the past and apply them in new settings with expanded meaning. For instance, the Xhosa word *ubuntu* is roughly translated as "a person is a person through other persons," and the term has been used to describe the value of sharing and the dependency we have on each other. The term may be used in multiple settings, such as when people are gathered around a common plate of food—where we will all share the same food and be nourished equally—or in the modern political context where it may be used to encourage nation building (Schneider 2002:55–57).

For some oral historians, the emergence of potential interpretation outside the historic context of intended meaning is a distortion, a leap from original intent. This leads some to search for original intent, the "most accurate" rendering of the story. This reductionist approach can lead to considerable loss of meaning as the researcher searches for consistency and agreement. This is where Foley and Cohen's work becomes so important. They recognize that stories operate within an historic and cultural context that

Photo by Jarrod Decker, courtesy of Denali Mountaineering Project Jukebox, www.uaf.edu/library/jukebox

This photo is of dog musher Will Forsberg (on the right) telling Bill Schneider (on the left) about his experiences freighting supplies by dog team to mountain climbers on Denali.

must be fully described and appreciated, but they also recognize that stories are fluid; they can be used in more than one way and can convey a range of meanings depending on context. For Cohen the range is ever-expanding and most important for him is to discern how the story takes on meaning over time. He celebrates the way people give stories wings to take off and meet the needs of new occasions. But what about the tape-recorded interview?

The tape recording represents history-making at one point in time (Dunaway and Baum 1996:8), an account crafted for an occasion and recorded for posterity. Once created, the record is much like the ancient texts, and our focus turns to understanding the context of that telling in relation to previous tellings, Foley's "tagged potentials." When there are future tellings, then we must extend our analysis to the record of how the story has been used, what we can learn about its intended meaning through time. Recordings and texts are static entities, unlike the story that is recreated with and for each new telling (Finnegan 1998:2). The meaning can only be fully understood against other accounts, some recorded, some not. The tape can be replayed and we can recall a past telling, but without a storyteller, that is, someone who chooses to re-tell the story, our reference is limited to how it has been used as opposed to its role in creating meaning in the present. Of course, our recall of the story in our minds is a form of personal storytelling, of re-creating meaning for the present. And, this is the first step in actually re-telling a story to others. People need to decide to retell the story, to make meaning in the present with the story. Oral performance is the way people choose to create and re-create meaning in the stories they tell and in the ways they interpret and retell them. The telling or performance becomes a critical part of not only the form, but the content, the substance of the story (Bauman and Briggs 1990; Toelken 1996, 117–33.); it is also the place where there is opportunity for innovation and change.

Swameji, a holy man who is the subject of Kirin Narayan's book *Storytellers, Saints, and Scoundrels*, instructed his followers: "You should never assign a meaning to a myth because if you assign a meaning, the mind clamps onto just that one meaning. Then it's no longer active because when a story is active it allows for new beginnings all the time" (1989:106). Swameji's instructions through stories provided his followers an array of settings and contexts to understand how to live. Many of his stories are quite familiar to his followers, but they took on new meaning each time he used them. Narayan and other followers of his teachings learned to live with his stories.

Of course, for those of us who are also curators of collections, we must not only understand how stories are used over time (live with stories), we must also preserve and make accessible the record that is produced. We have a responsibility to understand what we are preserving, the way it has been created, and how it is interpreted within historic and cultural contexts. Therefore, our challenge goes beyond material preservation and access to documentation and preservation of the recording contexts. That's our responsibility. Our opportunity is to listen to the story as it is told today and to draw upon multiple recordings of the story made over time to understand how it has been used (Hatang 2000; Hamilton et al. 2002; Schneider 2002:161–167). This collection of essays is offered as a way to demonstrate how that scholarship can be done.

Origins of This Collection

The main plenary session for the 2004 U.S. Oral History Association meetings featured a discussion of Alessandro Portelli's new book, *The Order has Been Carried Out*, a study of the oral accounts and written record of a Nazi massacre in Rome.[2] The massacre story, as it has been told over the years, is a key to the political attitudes and modern history of Italy. In her remarks at the symposium on Portelli's book, Paula Hamilton captured this sentiment when she credited Portelli's work with exploring "ways of taking the past forward which emerge from the idea that the present is obliged to accommodate the past in order to move on from itself" (2005:14). In the tradition of Ives, Santora, Allen, Cruikshank, Cohen, and Foley, Portelli's work demonstrates not only that a population is living with a story that has an historic and cultural context that can be understood, but also how this story shapes their lives and attitudes towards each other today.

So, when the invitation came to organize a special session on storytelling at that same meeting, I jumped at the chance. The time was ripe to bring together a group of scholars who would explore how stories challenge us to understand their meaning in context and their evolution over time, the essence of issues raised by Cohen, Foley, and Portelli and the challenge faced by all who work with stories.

Now, two years after that conference, with most of our original contributors and some additions, we hope to continue to build on the theme that we truly do live with stories in our lives and to demonstrate through case studies and discussions some of the ways that stories are important. Each author in this volume traces a story and the circumstances of its retelling. The authors situate their discussion of variations in each retelling to indicate how we are influenced to remember and how we choose to retell. Each essay is followed by dialogue with a second scholar who extends the discussion to their work with narrative.

In Holly Cusack-McVeigh's piece, an important place, the Giant Footsteps, leads Yup'ik Eskimo villagers to recall a well-known narrative and the lessons they were taught about the importance of proper behavior. McVeigh traces when and how she was told about this place and the lessons she learned from each telling. Her discussant, Klara Kelley, works with Navajo and finds the Yup'ik way that current events can become part of a traditional story to be in contrast to what she has learned from the Navajo, where the old stories must maintain their integrity and where one's current experiences are referenced outside the formal story. For the Yup'ik residents of Hooper Bay, the Giant Footsteps are a close visual reminder of the moral order; for the Navajo, the ceremonial stories describe the ancient sites but the meaning of the sites is not as easily accessible, particularly to children who have left the homeland for school or other reasons and aren't present at the ceremonies where they would learn about the sites. In both cases, the author and commentator note that it is an increasingly difficult challenge to instruct young people about places, stories, and their meaning.

Joanne Mulcahy's essay focuses on the use of metaphor in a Mexican American woman's oral narratives. Metaphors about trees, their bark, and leaves are a common theme in Eva Castellanoz' stories and are a familiar link back to her Mexican oral tradition where the Tree of Life is a central cultural symbol. Mulcahy traces Castellanoz' use of the tree metaphor to describe her mother's work as a healer and her own work with at-risk youth. The essay demonstrates how the constancy of the metaphor can be a familiar frame for the narrator to shape lessons about health and social well-being. For the Mexican American audience, the metaphor is a touchstone to their heritage, a visual and familiar link to the themes under consideration. Metaphors are a building block of narrative, and in this essay we see how important the blocks are in the construction of stories. Barbara Babcock, the discussant, extends the conversation through comparative perspectives on Pueblo storytelling as a "generative" force, passing on the culture while bringing the community together. Babcock and Mulcahy's conversation also turns to gender issues in fieldwork and in cultural representation. Both authors point out how intimate and personal their work is and how it calls for new ways of expressing and writing about their experiences.

Kirin Narayan's essay describes her reintroduction of an Indian song to a group of Indian women in a village in the Himalayan foothills. Years before, Narayan recorded a women's song about Krishna's encounter with a beautiful woman. The song was familiar to the women gathered for a wedding but there were verses to the song that they did not know. In Narayan's description of her reintroduction of the song, we see how this song is part of a traditional set of wedding songs that are sung when young girls go off to their future husband's village to marry. The women are expected to sing the song, but because they come from different villages they may not know all of the verses. The discussant for this piece is Barre Toelken, who points out how songs, with their melody, rhyme, and familiar verses, act as mechanisms to enhance the learning of new verses interspersed with the familiar. He relates the song tradition to his own experiences coming from an East Coast commercial whaling family, where certain songs are a common bond among family members and evoke strong emotion. Narayan sees her example of the wedding songs and Toelken's description of the whaling songs as examples of storytelling that provides "a strong sense of continuity with our progenitors."

Aron Crowell and Estelle Oozevaseuk's essay was inspired by a visit of St. Lawrence Island Yupik[3] Eskimo elders to the Smithsonian Institution to work with heritage objects in the museum's collections. There, a gut skin parka was the inspiration for Estelle Oozevaseuk to retell the story of the St. Lawrence Island famine and epidemic of 1878–80. Her story, unlike written accounts by government officials, describes how hunters mistreated a walrus by skinning it alive and how because of this transgression the people of the community had to die. However, their deaths lead to a form of resurrection to a better life. The authors' description of the discrepancies in interpretation about what caused the famine leads us to reflect on the way some members of the community have made sense, in their own minds, of the disaster. Discussant James Clifford points out how stories are never limited to just facts but are also opportunities to point to deeper meanings that go beyond a strict rendering of what "actually" happened. In this case, the Western written sources claim the cause of the disaster to have been alcohol abuse and a poor walrus hunt, whereas the account given by Oozevaseuk emphasizes the breach of moral and spiritual relationship with the walrus and the consequences of this act. Christian and traditional beliefs are interwoven in her account, which emphasizes that people must live respectfully with the resources they have been given and there are severe consequences for neglecting these responsibilities, but in admitting transgression there is promise for salvation.

Sherna Gluck's essay takes us to Palestine, the development of the women's movement there, and how it both contributed to and was impacted by the first *intifada*. She points out that the emphasis in the way the story is told shifts over time according to the political climate. Context and audience are key factors that determine the emphasis placed on certain parts of the larger story. Gluck alerts us to the fact that the story may change its emphasis according to the political climate, but this does not necessarily mean the story has lost parts of its original meaning. Gluck's commentator, Ted Swedenburg, invites us to recognize the power of "official narrative" and how it functions in accounts such as the Palestinian women's story to overpower other renderings of the narrative. He poses the example of Vietnam veterans and how a public story emerged about how they were treated on their return, a story that became the "official" interpretation, despite evidence to the contrary. Gluck adds additional perspective on the complexity of relating "official stories" to individual retellings in a description of her interviews with garment workers in the United States. In that case, she points out how growing trust with a narrator allowed the teller to feel comfortable diverting from the "official story." The essay is a reminder that our growing relationship with our narrators provides perspective on how they use a story at any particular telling and how powerful political forces can shape and influence the record produced.

The last essay by Lorraine McConaghy describes how she reintroduces oral history accounts to museum visitors so that they can experience aspects of Seattle history that have not been told in the "official record." Visitors are asked to read portions of transcripts and take on a character who describes his or her experiences. Visitors are forced to imagine what their character experienced and to relate it to their lives. Karen Utz is the discussant. She is the curator at Sloss Furnace National Historic Landmark, where she has also used oral history narratives in the schools to teach students about Birmingham industrial history. McConnaghy and Utz' discussion leads us to consider how reenactments are a way to extend the less well-known historical accounts to a public audience and how the act of voicing a character can create a personal connection with that character and their experiences.

In each of our explorations into retellings, we are reminded that the present is a key to how and what we remember. An ancient site is a reminder of how to behave. The needs of the present prompt the Mexican American healer to frame with familiar metaphor the story that heals. The parka at the Smithsonian is a prompt to retell the story of its origin and its significance in an historic tragedy. The Palestinian narrators feel the constraints of the present political environment as they shape their narratives of the women's role in the *intifada*. The group of women gathered for the Indian wedding is the context where Narayan reintroduces the traditional song, and the group joins in the verses they know and collectively re-create the song that enriches their wedding event. McConaghy invites her visitors to participate in the narratives of the past, and the process forces them to confront their own experiences and lives today as they try to understand and portray the character they have been asked to present.

Each essay reminds us that if we are open to how retellings can be influenced by the present, if we are willing to live with stories, then memory becomes more than a vessel of information and detail that we accurately or inaccurately, completely or incompletely, draw upon. Memory is also a response to the moment: information that we need to recall because it relates to the present. The present, as Hamilton put it, is "obliged to accommodate the past in order to move on from itself." And story making is the way we draw from the past to serve the present and future.

Notes

1. It is interesting to note that Ives' video *An Oral Historian's Work* (2005) is still the flagship introduction to the field after nineteen years. His contributions were formally recognized in a special session at the 2005 Oral History Association meeting. For many years, Barbara Allen and Lynwood Montell's book *From Memory to History* (1981) was a classic primer for oral history research.
2. Portelli, a professor of American literature in Rome, was recipient of the 2004 best book award by the Oral History Association.
3. The spellings *Yup'ik*, used by Cusack-McVeigh and *Yupik*, used by Crowell and Oozevaseuk, reflect linguistic differences among Eskimo groups.

References

Allen, Barbara, and William Lynwood Montell. 1981. *From Memory to History: Using Oral Sources in Local Historical Research*. Nashville. The American Association for State and Local History.

Baum, Willa. 1983. The Other Uses of Oral History. In *Sharing Alaska's Oral History*, 37–51. Proceedings of the Conference held at the Captain Cook Hotel, Anchorage, Alaska, October 26–27, 1982. Compiled by William Schneider, University of Alaska Fairbanks.

Bauman, Richard, and Charles Briggs. 1990. Poetics and Performance as Critical Perspectives on Language and Social Life. In *Annual Review of Anthropology* 19: 59–88.

Blythe, Ronald. 1969. *Akenfield: Portrait of an English Village*. New York: Pantheon.

Bogart, Barbara Allen. 1995. *In Place: Stories of Landscape and Identity from the American West*. Glendo, WY: High Plains Press.

Brown, Jennifer. 1991. Ethnohistorians: Strange Bedfellows, Kindred Spirits. *Ethnohistory* 38(2): 113–23.

Brown, Jennifer and Elizabeth Vibert. 2003. *Reading Beyond Words: Contexts for Native History*. Peterborough, Ontario: Broadview Press.

Cohen, David William. 1994. *The Combing of History*. Chicago: University of Chicago Press.

Cruikshank, Julie. 1990. *Life Lived Like a Story: Life Stories of Three Yukon Native Elders*. Lincoln: University of Nebraska Press.

———. 1995. "Pete's Song": Establishing Meanings through Story and Song. In *When our Words Return: Writing, Hearing, and Remembering Oral Traditions of Alaska and the Yukon*, Phyllis Morrow and William Schneider, eds., 53–75.

———. 1998. *The Social Life of Stories: Narrative and Knowledge in the Yukon Territory*. Lincoln: University of Nebraska Press.

Dunaway, David. 1991. The Oral Biography. *Biography* 14(3): 256–66.

Dunaway, David, and Willa Baum (eds.). 1996. *Oral History: An Interdisciplinary Anthology*. Walnut Creek, CA: Altamira Press.

Finnegan, Ruth. 1998. *Oral Literature in Africa*. Oxford: Oxford University Press.

———. 1992. *Oral Tradition and the Verbal Arts*. London: Routledge.

Foley, John Miles. 1995. *The Singer of Tales in Performance*. Bloomington: Indiana University Press.

———. 2005 (April 15). Excavating an Epic, on oral tradition and the internet, otandit.blogspot.com/.

Gluck, Sherna. 1987. *Rosie the Riveter Revisited: Women, the War, and Social Change*. Boston: Twayne.

Hamilton, Carolyn, Jane Taylor, Graeme Reid, Michele Pickover, Razia Saleh, and Verne Harris (eds.). 2002. Living by Fluidity: Oral Histories, Material Custodies, and the Politics of Archiving. In *Refiguring the Archive*, 209–28. Cape Town: David Philip Publishers.

Hamilton, Paula. 2005. The Oral Historian as Memorist. *Oral History Review* 32(1): 11–18.

Hareven, Tamara. 1978. *Amoskeag: Life and Work in an American Factor-city*. New York: Pantheon.

Hatang, Sello. 2000. Converting Orality to Material Custody: Is it a Noble act of Liberation or is it an Act of Incarceration? *Escarbica Journal* 19: 22–30.

Henige, David. 1982. *Oral Historiography*. London: Langman.

Hymes, Dell. 1981. *"In Vain I Tried to Tell You": Essays in Native American Ethnopoetics*. Philadelphia: University of Pennsylvania Press.

Ives, Edward. 1988. *George Magoon and the Down East Game War: History, Folklore, and the Law*. Urbana, IL: University of Chicago Press.

———. 2005. *An Oral Historian's Work*. [video recording]. Produced by Northeast Archives of Folklore and Oral History, University of Maine. Bucksport: Northeast Historic Films.

Kline, Carrie Nobel. 1996. Giving it Back: Creating Conversations to Interpret Community Oral History. *Oral History Review* 19: 9–39.

Krech, Shepard. 1991. The State of Ethnohistory. *Annual Review of Anthropology* 20: 345–75.

Langness, Lewis and Gelya Frank. 1981. *Lives: An Anthropological Approach to Biography*. Novato: Chandler and Sharp Publishers.

Lewin, Rhoda, ed. 1990. *Witnesses to the Holocaust: An Oral History*. Boston: Twayne.

Lewis, Oscar. 1965. *La Vida*. New York: Random House.

Lurie, Nancy. 1961. *Mountain Wolf Woman, Sister of Crashing Thunder: The Autobiography of a Winnebago Indian*. Ann Arbor: University of Michigan Press.

Mintz, Sidney. 1960. *Worker in the Cane: A Puerto Rican Life History*. New Haven: Yale University Press.

Narayan, Kirin. 1989. *Storytellers, Saints, and Scoundrels: Folk Narrative in Hindu Religious Teaching*. Philadelphia: University of Pennsylvania Press.

Portelli, Alessandro. 2003. *The Order has Been Carried Out: History, Memory, and Meaning of a Nazi Massacre in Rome*. New York: Palgrave MacMillan.

Radin, Paul. 1963. *The Autobiography of a Winnebago Indian*. New York: Dover.

Ritchie, Donald. 1987. Oral History and the Federal Government. *Journal of American History* 74(2): 587–95.

———. 1995. *Doing Oral History*. New York: Twayne.

Rogovin, Milton, and Michael Frisch. 1993. *Portraits in Steel*. Ithaca, NY: Cornell University Press.

Rosengarten, Theodore. 1974. *All God's Dangers: The Life of Nate Shaw*. New York: Alfred Knopf.

Santino, Jack. 1989. *Miles of Smiles, Years of Struggle: Stories of Black Pullman Porters*. Urbana, IL: University of Illinois Press.

Schneider, William. 2002. ... *So They Understand: Cultural Issues in Oral History*. Logan: Utah State University Press.

———. 2003. The Search for Wisdom in Native American Narratives and Classical Scholarship. *Oral Tradition Slavica* 18(2): 268–69.

Sturtevant, William. 1966. Anthropology, History, and Ethnohistory. *Ethnohistory* 13(12):1–51.

Tamura, Linda. 1993. *The Hood River Issei: An Oral History of Japanese Settlers in Oregon's Hood River Valley*. Urbana, IL: University of Illinois Press.

Terkel, Studs. 1984. *"The Good War": An Oral History of World War Two*. New York: Pantheon.

Thompson, Paul. 2000. *The Voice of the Past, Oral History*. Oxford: Oxford University Press.

Thomson, Alistair. 2007. Four Paradigm Transformations in Oral History. *Oral History Review* 34(1):49–70.

Titon, Jeff Todd. 1980. The Life Story. *Journal of American Folklore* 93(369): 276–92.

Toelken, Barre. 1996. *The Dynamics of Folklore*. Logan: Utah State University Press.

Trouillot, Michel-Rolph. 1995. *Silencing the Past: Power and the Production of History*. Boston: Beacon Press.

Vansina, Jan. 1965. *Oral Tradition: A Study in Historical Methodology*. London: Routledge.

2

The Giant Footprints

A Lived Sense of Story and Place

Holly Cusack-McVeigh

Holly Cusack-McVeigh is a research anthropologist and adjunct professor of anthropology at the University of Alaska's Kenai Peninsula College. Her most recent research explores oral history and folklore on the Bering Sea Coast. In this essay, she retraces her experiences hearing "The Giant Footprints," a Yup'ik Eskimo story from the village of Hooper Bay. The story relates how two young girls disappeared into the land when they failed to follow proper menstrual practices. The place where this occurred is a constant, tangible reminder of how to act, and the story of the girls is retold to reinforce these cultural lessons. The author carefully recorded the settings in which she was told the story and how people were using the story to teach her about Yup'ik culture and beliefs.

On the shore of the Bering Sea, between the mouths of the Yukon and Kuskokwim rivers, lies the Yup'ik Eskimo village of Hooper Bay. In the early 1840s L. A. Zagoskin, a Russian naval lieutenant, wrote that the people of this region were known as Magmyut, "those who lived on the level tundra places" (Michael 1967:210). E. W. Nelson, an American naturalist for the Smithsonian Institution, also wrote about this place as he traveled throughout the region collecting natural history specimens and material culture. At the time of

18

Courtesy of James H. Barker

Yup'ik Village on the Yukon-Kuskokwim Delta.

Nelson's 1878 visit, Hooper Bay was known as Askinuk. Few outsiders had come to this part of the Yukon-Kuskokwim Delta before Nelson's arrival. The 1890 census report states that "the inhabitants are *Magmiuts,* 138 in number, who live in 14 dwellings and 2 *kashgas* [ceremonial houses]" (Report on the Population and Resources of Alaska at the 11th Census, 1890:111).

Much has changed in Hooper Bay since Nelson's visit. The present-day village is one of the largest villages in Alaska, with well over a thousand community members. In spite of a tumultuous history and the impact of dramatic change (Napoleon 1991), the oral traditions continue to be a central aspect of contemporary life. Among Yupiit, places and their stories serve as a reference, barometer, and guide.

During my first week in Hooper Bay, now more than ten years ago, a group of young men invited me to go set nets in the mouth of the river across the bay. I had come to their village to contextualize an archival photographic collection. Consequently, I had spent many hours working and visiting with their grandmother, a respected community elder. I jumped at the chance to get out and explore. Their family loaned me a pair of waders and we set off for the row of skiffs lined up along the shoreline. It was a wonderful day and we all enjoyed being "out on the land." We set several nets, walked the beaches where we discovered the carcass of a large whale, and took turns at target practice with a .22 rifle. On our

Courtesy of James H. Barker

Men departing for a seal hunt.

return trip a seal presented itself in the bay.[1] After a lengthy pursuit we finally gave up when it lead us out into the rough, choppier waters of the open sea. I recall my deep disappointment as this, my first "seal hunt," had ended in failure. I silently questioned the experience and skill of these young hunters. After all, we had lost the seal, prized for both its delicious meat and seal oil.[2]

When we reached the village shore we began gathering up our nets and other supplies. As we worked to unload the skiff one of them asked, "Have you seen the giant footprints?" When I replied that I had not, they quickly offered to take me to this place on the tundra. We jumped onto their four-wheelers and headed out onto the tundra, making our way up the coast. As we approached I could easily see them at a distance: large, deep depressions extending out before us. I was anxious to get down and examine them closer, but I was teasingly warned by these young men not to step directly into these footprints. I cautiously and respectfully walked around them, although I didn't fully understand why.

One of the first stories I ever heard in Hooper Bay is tied to this particular place on the tundra. The story of "The Giant Footprints" recalls how the people were holding a feast and dancing down at the old village site of Askinuk. As was the custom, two young girls who had just begun menstruation were left behind. The sound of singing and drumming enticed the young girls to sneak out and head towards the celebration. Tellers often explicitly state that the girls disregarded what they knew to be appropriate behavior.[3] Tellers go on to describe the excitement of the young girls as they headed towards the ceremony, but as they crossed the tundra the ground began to "roll" and move. At this point, one teller explained to me that the "earth used to be much thinner" than it is today. As the girls tried to make their way towards the celebration, they started to sink. The more they struggled, the more they sank down. They sank into the tundra and became lost to the world of the living. They became a part of another world, a world that is not entirely separate from the world of the living, but they were never seen again.

Every version that I have been told of "The Giant Footprints"[4] is similar in content. This narrative emphasizes that these young girls had just begun puberty. The tellers often stop to explicitly explain to me that, in traditional Yup'ik Eskimo belief, girls should not go out in public or dance during their time of menstruation.[5] It was customary for girls to remain indoors and away from the rest of the family and community members during this time. Nelson himself wrote that "a particular atmosphere is supposed to surround her at this time, and if a young man should come near enough for it to touch him it would render him visible to every animal he might hunt, so that his own success as a hunter would be gone" (Nelson 1983 [1899]: 291).

A Jesuit missionary at Hooper Bay during the 1930s wrote that "while menstruation is going on she is not allowed to leave the house but has to hide herself in one corner of the igloo [sod house]. And if the family just happens to have to move camp while she is in this condition she has to be laid in the sled and covered up so that she can not see anything, nor touch the ground. If she would touch the ground hunters would have bad luck, and spirits would likely take her soul away" (AM Collection 30:1105–1213).

In May of 2000 I worked with community members on a project entitled "Sharing Our Traditions: Searching for Meaning." The tribal council met to discuss this project and the following month, in June of 2000, I returned again to help carry out the objectives outlined in the proposal. This time I traveled to Hooper Bay with my six–year-old son. One day my son and I were walking to the store when one of the council members, another community elder, stopped us. My son eagerly ran off to play with a group of children while we visited and talked about the project. As we watched the kids playing nearby, this man spoke of other Hooper Bay elders

he thought should be included in the project. With what seemed
to be an abrupt shift in our conversation, he began to talk about
the giant footprints. As he spoke, he pointed to the open tundra
behind me where the deep depressions mark the land. He told me
the story of the young girls and explained to me that those giant
footprints were out there on the land today.

Like previous tellings I had heard, he explained that the footprints were made by two young girls who had ignored the wisdom
of their elders. They had not respected the Yup'ik behavioral rules
regarding menstruation. I was, admittedly, intrigued by one aspect
of his story in which the girls "are now up in the sky." I immediately recalled Nelson's writings in which he had described a "sky
land" in reference to Yup'ik stories of Raven (Nelson 1983 [1899]).
I wondered how this fit with the girls being taken into the land. I
must have let my curiosity show because he seemed to know that
this tale had piqued my interest. Smiling at me he stated "you will
hear about that one." Nodding his head with assurance he told me
again, "You will hear more about them [the giant footprints]!" We
then parted company. I found my son and we were once again off
to the store.

As we made our way up the hill toward the old part of the village, I wished that I had taken this opportunity to ask him more
about this narrative. I thought, "I missed my chance *again!*" Then,
laughing to myself, I recalled the lesson I had learned so many
times before. As folklorists Phyllis Morrow and William Schneider
remind their readers, "words return." Stories and narratives, like
the seals who have been hunted and killed, return to those who
demonstrate respect and patience (Morrow and Schneider 1995).
Words return as stories to find *you!*

While conducting archival research, I discovered that this narrative had also been shared with Helen Oswalt (then a University of
Alaska Fairbanks graduate student) when she visited Hooper Bay
back in 1950. Her field notes state that:

> Once there was very thin land here. Two girls were left in [a] hut
> their family built for their puberty (they wore hoods) while rest of vil-
> lage went to sealing camp. Girls heard dance music, [and] knew they
> weren't allowed to go but wanted to. All who go to dances must take
> something [an offering] so they took the leftak [sic] skin from the
> doorway and started out with it between them. After walking a while,
> they began sinking in the shallow ground and then began going up to

the sky. They started back another way, and the same thing happened. They disappeared in [the] sky, but footsteps can still be seen here. (Oswalt 1951:11)

This 1950 telling is strikingly similar in detail to the versions that have been shared with me over the years by various tellers at Hooper Bay, except that here sinking into the ground and ascending into the sky were again linked in the same telling. The elder who shared this story with me when we met on the road had said, "you will hear more about them," and he was right. Later that same year, I would find myself sitting with another well-respected elder as we recorded his life history, and he too would weave this narrative of the "Giant Footprints" into his own story. He smiled with pride as he recalled the place where he got his first seal as a young boy and he described the many places on the tundra where he had learned to hunt birds with his grandfather. He recalled, too, the many times he had passed those giant footprints. He then shared this story of the young girls before turning back to his own personal narrative. This is an important feature of storytelling in Hooper Bay. People connect their own life story to places on the land and in doing so connect the stories of place to their own experiences. It is an integral part of Yup'ik belief and sense of place. Hastrup, in recording life histories in an Icelandic community, has similarly noted this aspect of oral tradition in relation to place. She writes that "we were not only met with a life history, but also a life space" (Hastrup 1998:112).

In October of 2001, a Hooper Bay community member and I decided to give a paper at the annual meeting of the American Folklore Society held in Anchorage, Alaska. The theme of the conference was "partners in knowledge." We were invited to participate in a session that explored "The Power of Alaskan Places." We had recently conducted a recorded interview with another community elder who had shared with us the story of "The Giant Footprints." We decided to ask this particular elder to join us in our presentation. What proved to be most valuable was the time that the three of us spent together preparing for our public presentation.

As we sat in an empty conference room at the Hilton Hotel, we listened to this elder tell the story of "The Giant Footprints" as she planned to tell it to our larger, intended audience. What was most fascinating was the way that she embedded, in this widely known tale, her personal narrative. As she described the young

Mapping place names and place narratives, 2001.

girls sinking down into the earth she suddenly turned to her own story and a similar experience that she had with this sentient land. Her story, also, seemed to highlight the important relationship of respect for a sentient land.

She began her story by telling us of a young boy in Hooper Bay whom she had cured with water found at a special location on the tundra. This small boy had suffered an illness that resulted in a serious affliction of his arms, neck, trunk, and face. She described how she went to this place on the tundra to collect the water to heal this child. She explained to us that she wanted to thank the land (*nuna*) for the healing waters and that she felt she had so little to offer. She tells us, her listeners, that she had thought about it for a long time and finally decided that she would offer, as a gift, her sewing needle. This was, indeed, a significant gift, as she is well-known and admired for her sewing and basket making even to this day.

She reenacts the careful placement of the bone needle as though she is doing it at the very moment of her telling. She explains to us that sometimes the land will reject a gift, not accept it from the people who offer it. She laughs uncomfortably as she recalls how very nervous she felt as she gently placed the bone needle down into the tundra waters. Her hand still extended out, she stares ahead as though she is there now, nervously watching it as it floats on the surface of the water. As she tells this story, her eyes remain fixed on a single object. She does not see us (her listeners) or the empty conference room where we are sitting. She is watching that needle float. She is waiting to see if this gift will be accepted. Her face lights up suddenly as she describes her great relief and joy at the sight of the needle slowly disappearing under the water. She knows that her gift of thanks has been accepted. "Oh, I was *so* happy!" she says as she fondly remembers this powerful life experience. This narrative, like the story of "The Giant Footprints," gives us a sense of a complex and overlapping world. It also beautifully illustrates the ongoing relationship of reciprocity and respect that Yupiit maintain with the land and also how stories are embedded in life experience. In this case, the giant footprints serve as a springboard for this teller's personal story of her own interaction with the land and the acceptance of her gift.

One of the most recent tellings of "The Giant Footprints" was shared with me in the fall of 2002 during a recorded interview. Interestingly, this telling would also be linked to another narrative that was very similar in content and form. This particular community elder stated that his grandfather and father often told him the story and that he would see the footprints at that place out on the land when he was hunting.

Elder: "I used to go bow and arrow, bird hunting" [at that place].

Holly: "Yeah, you would see them?"

Elder: "*Tamana*" [refers to that place spoken of. Out, over there, extended space].

Listener: "*Ii-I*" [yes, another listener who nods his head in agreement].

Elder: "Uh, growing up, [I would often see] those footsteps from these young girls, that just got into their [first time]. Two young girls that just started having their periods."

Elder: "They [the footprints] used to be deep when I was young, back then."

Elder: "When they went down to the dance, they say they went under the usual path; I think they went under the ground.

At this particular point in his telling he makes an abrupt leap from the tale of the giant footprints to another story. The story of the giant footprints becomes linked to a longer, embedded narrative in which a group of children also become lost in the land at a place he calls the Volcano Mountains. The teller states that these children "go *under* the ground." This occurs when they fail to listen to the important teachings of their elders, carelessly passing through the underground passageways during a ceremonial time.[6] This was a time when the human and spirit worlds were closer, a time when the boundaries between worlds were diminished.

> It is said that when they went into one of the houses, they missed the path that went into the house, but instead went under the path, in those *qasgi*. . . . They say they went out through the ground. . . . Yeah, they went below the underground entrance, when they tried to go in through the underground entrance, they began to travel through the ground underneath the tunnel.

Like the narrative of the giant footprints, this tale is about more than just getting lost on the land. The children become, for a time, a part of the land at this place known as the Volcano Mountains. This teller described the parents' anguish as they could hear their children crying for help but were unable to reach them. Morrow notes that this is a well-known Yup'ik story often told in connection with *Qaariitaaq*. She writes, "In this way, they [the lost children] acted like the spirits of the dead, who gathered under the *qasgi* for ceremonies when the people invited them to come from the under-world" (Morrow 1984:122). Unlike the girls who left the giant footprints, these children eventually resurface at the Volcano Mountain, returning to the world of the living. The teller explains that when they come out "they're really old, *really* old!" These two narratives are linked not only because they are similar in content. They are linked by their connection to particular places on the land, places that are aware and responsive. It seems to me that certain places hold a greater potential for human contact with the spirit world.

This became clear to me one day while out collecting driftwood with my friends. They offered to take me to the abandoned village site near the giant footprints. From both the air and ground, one can see the remains of large, dome-shaped semisubterranean sod houses where the Hooper Bay ancestors once lived. I was eager to explore this abandoned village site and quickly climbed one of the earthen mounds. I was even able to crawl through an opening that once served as a tunnel, doorway entrance. Slightly collapsed, the wooden support beam was still in place and, although it was a tight squeeze, I managed to crawl through the passageway of this dwelling. Nelson described these passageways at Askinuk in great detail, stating that:

> The houses are clustered together in the most irregular manner, and the entrances to the passageways leading to the interiors open out in the most unexpected places. Sometimes one of these passages opens on the top of another house built lower down on the side of the mound, or, it may be, between two houses, or almost against the side of an adjoining one. (Nelson 1983 [1899]:249)

Passing through this entryway was a momentary event, but one I would always remember. As I crawled through this passageway I had a strong sense of touching history, but I immediately noticed that this made my Yup'ik companions very uneasy. At the time I did not understand why this would make people so uncomfortable. I was truly puzzled by their look of concern. I even examined the structure, wondering if it was unsafe. I just could not understand why they seemed so uneasy with my actions. I also wondered why the Hooper Bay ancestors had left this place.[7] At the time, I lacked the cultural contextualization that narratives of place provide and thus the knowledge of how to act appropriately. After several years and many more stories, I would come to understand their sentiment better. I would also, through narratives of place, come to see my own actions as foolish and careless.

I have heard the story of "The Giant Footprints" told many times over the years. Each telling explains how these footprints came to be. The place of the giant footprints exists as a tangible and concrete reminder of deeply rooted Yup'ik knowledge and shared contemporary values. Each telling and each allusion to this place reinforces the importance of respecting the wisdom of community elders. These tellings underscore the importance of Yup'ik knowledge by highlighting the potentially serious effects of dismissing it. Clearly, the story of "The Giant Footprints" is an important one that continues to hold meaning for the people of Hooper Bay. This narrative, as well as the story of "The Children Who Came Out at the Volcano Mountains" and the narrative in which the elder gives "A Gift to the Land" all demonstrate that the landscape is much more than an inanimate place. Human beings are not separate and distinct from the natural world but are instead very much a part of it. This sense of place includes the world of spirits and other beings who inhabit the tundra, the waters, and other features of the world around them.

This is a lived "sense of place" where wisdom sits in places (Basso 1996). These places remind Yupiit of their cultural values and beliefs, but they also react to human behavior. The land, in essence, is a social actor capable of directly responding to human actions. Like the seals who are hunted and those of the spirit world, places on the land are always watching and aware. Like people and other creatures, the land responds both positively and negatively, depending on the context of the particular event or human action. The needle was accepted and brought joy to the land. The elder who linked the Volcano Mountains story to the giant footprints also informs his audience that "they [the footprints] used to be deep when I was young back then." I strongly suspect that this description of the changing depth of the footprints parallels the many descriptions of an often "thicker" land in contemporary times. This "thickness," I am told, has decreased the permeability between the contemporary human and spirit worlds. A thicker land[8] and diminishing footprints are both signs of a world that is not well.[9] There is a sense that when the community is not well, the land and spirit world are not well. Perhaps the earth's thickness and diminished land features are in direct response to diminished awareness and sensitivity to the spirit world?

The giant footprints, the actual depressions, are cognizant of human actions and continue to inform people. They hold symbolic import, serving as a tangible reminder of the importance of Yup'ik teachings and belief for community members but simultaneously serving as a strong cautionary tale for outsiders who lack the knowledge to behave properly.[10] Thus, those giant footprints reinforce the fact that the world can also be a dangerous place for those non-Yupiit who do not respect Yup'ik ways.

It has been more than ten years since that seal eluded us. Then I questioned the young hunters' skills, but now I have come to believe that my very presence, as a female, is a more plausible explanation for its loss. Women today, as in the past, don't typically go out seal hunting with men. I now believe that I was led to those giant footprints for a particular reason. Within a Yup'ik context, the telling was both an explanation for the loss of the seal and a cautionary tale for this then-newcomer. It took almost a decade for me to understand why this story may have been shared with me that long ago July evening. As in much of Yup'ik instruction, I was not told what to learn from my experience or the story. I was left to find meaning as my life unfolds.

The way that places are consulted for guidance is characteristic of the Yupiit of Southwestern Alaska. The land is a being among beings, and a particularly powerful and sensitive one. For Yupiit in Hooper Bay, places and stories are not simply symbolic, they are active elements of social life. As Elsie Mather, a respected Yup'ik educator, reminds us, "storytelling is part of the action of living" (Morrow and Schneider 1995:33).

Notes

1. Yupiit believe that game animals "present" and give themselves to those who demonstrate respect and proper behavior (Hensel 1996).
2. Hensel (1996) notes that seal oil remains a highly valued food item throughout the Yup'ik region.
3. This motif (girls who have just had their first period and are tempted by curiosity) is a common prelude to trouble in Yup'ik Eskimo stories (Morrow 2002).
4. Alternately referred to as "giant footsteps."
5. Morrow notes that numerous rules guided women's behavior at menarche (Morrow 2002).
6. This ceremony was identified as *qaariitaaq* (also the contemporary word for Halloween), but as linguist Steve Jacobson notes *qaariitaaq* was a Yup'ik ceremony that predated contact (Jacobson 1984:302). Phyllis Morrow (1984) and Elsie Mather (1985) identify *qaariitaaq* ("going in and out of houses") as the first of many ceremonies that preceded the Bladder Festival.
7. Epidemics forced the abandonment of villages throughout Alaska. Hooper Bay community member Harold Napoleon writes that his ancestors were "too weak to bury all the dead" and that "many survivors abandoned the old villages, some caving in their houses with the dead still in them. Their homeland—the tundra, the Bering Sea coast, the riverbanks—had become a dying field for the Yup'ik people" (Napoleon 1991:11).
8. The thickness of the earth today is not static. There is still the potential for a change in the thickness of the land in response to human actions, but perhaps less often than in times past. In a personal communication with Phyllis Morrow (2006) she stated that she has also heard that the earth becomes "thinner or thicker in response to that relationship."
9. I have often encountered talk of diminished land features in the form of metaphoric speech. For example, one teller, who wished to avoid direct talk of painful events, abruptly stated that the tundra ponds don't have as much water as they once did and that there are no more flowers on the land.
10. What Keith Basso (1979) refers to as "blundering fools" in Western Apache storytelling.

References

AM Collection, Alaska Mission Collection. John P. Fox, S. J., Collection, Microfilm Roll 30. Oregon Province Archives of the Society of Jesus. Gonzaga University, Spokane, Washington.

Basso, Keith H. 1979. *"Portraits of the Whiteman": Linguistic Play and Cultural Symbols Among the Western Apache.* Cambridge: Cambridge University Press.

———. 1996 *Wisdom Sits in Places: Landscape and Language Among the Western Apache.* Albuquerque: University of New Mexico Press.

Hastrup, Kirsten. 1997. *A Place Apart: An Anthropological Study of the Icelandic World.* Oxford: Clarendon Press.

Hensel, Chase. 1996. *Telling Our Selves: Ethnicity and Discourse in Southwestern Alaska.* New York: Oxford University Press.

Jacobson, Steven A. 1984. *Yup'ik Eskimo Dictionary.* Fairbanks: Alaska Native Language Center.

Mather, Elsie. 1985. *Cauyarnariuq [A Time for Drumming].* Bethel, Alaska: Lower Kuskokwim School District.

Michael, Henry N. 1967. *Lieutenant Zagoskin's Travels in Russian America 1842–1844: The First Ethnographic and Geographic Investigations in the Yukon and Kuskokwim Valleys of Alaska.* Toronto: University of Toronto Press.

Morrow, Phyllis. 1984. It is Time for Drumming: A Summary of Recent Research on Yup'ik Eskimo Ceremonialism. In *The Central Yupik Eskimos,* supplementary issue *Etudes/Inuit/Studies,* vol. 8 edited by E. S. Burch, Jr., University of Laval, Quebec, Canada.

———. 2002 A Woman's Vapor: Yup'ik Bodily Powers in Southwest Alaska. *Ethnology* 41(4):335–48.

Morrow, Phyllis, and William Schneider, eds. 1995. *When Our Words Return: Writing, Hearing, and Remembering Oral Traditions of Alaska and the Yukon.* Logan: Utah State University Press.

Napoleon, Harold. 1991. *Yuuyaraq: The Way of the Human Being.* Fairbanks: Center for Cross-Cultural Studies, College of Rural Alaska, University of Alaska Fairbanks.

Nelson, Edward W. 1983 [1899]. *The Eskimo About Bering Strait.* Washington: Smithsonian Institution Press.

Oswalt, Helen. 1951. Ethnological Notes from Hooper Bay. Unpublished MS, Alaska and Polar Regions Department, University of Alaska Fairbanks.

U.S. Bureau of the Census. Report on the Population and Resources of Alaska at the 11th Census, 1890. United States Census Office. Washington, D.C., 1893.

The Giant Footprints

A Conversation with Holly Cusack-McVeigh and
Klara B. Kelley

Holly Cusack-McVeigh and Klara Kelley explore the
role of place in Yup'ik and Navajo oral tradition.
They discover that the contexts for sharing narrative
in both traditions are very different; Cusack-McVeigh
finds that her Yup'ik friends see sites like the Giant
Footprints as barometers of social well-being and they
share with each other how their experiences relate to
the traditional story and the site. Kelley, drawing on
work with her Navajo colleague, Harris Francis, indi-
cates that the Navajo sacred sites are described in a
rich oral tradition that is only told in winter and in the
context of ceremonies. Individual Navajo may relate
this knowledge to their experiences, but the tellings
of the ancient stories and of stories about personal
experience with the sites are separate. Young people
in Yup'ik and Navajo culture therefore have different
types of opportunities to learn, relate to, and participate in their oral traditions. Both Cusack-McVeigh
and Kelley acknowledge that there may be fewer
such opportunities in these cultures where youth are
reminded of the importance of the stories and where
they would hear the ancient accounts referenced.
Yup'ik elders express concerns over the impacts of
a rapidly changing world and, in the Navajo case,
children are often not on the reservations in winter
when the ceremonies are held and the stories told.

SCHNEIDER: I want to begin with something Holly said in her
last e-mail to me. She said that "place anchors memory" and so I
thought we should start with that and then see how new events get
associated with places in our memory. So Klara, when Holly says,

---

Klara B. Kelley is an anthropologist who has been working for many years
with Navajo people in the American Southwest. She has teamed with Harris
Francis, a Navajo cultural expert, to document the cultural meaning of
Navajo historic sites. They are the authors of *Navajo Sacred Places* (1994).

"place anchors memory," how does that relate to your experiences working with Navajo people?

KELLEY: Well, I think places are an anchor for personal and social memory. Of course, people have their own personal experiences, but because there are particular oral traditions that they have been taught to remember in detail, and because these have been handed down through many generations in a particular way, these form what we might think of as a landscape constructed by many generations. Navajo people relate their personal experiences to that ceremonial landscape, and that kind of reinforces the ties between personal experience and the oral traditions of their society, the past and the present. But personal experiences don't get mixed into or retold as part of the oral tradition that is recounted in the ceremonies.

What has always been emphasized for those of us who do research here in Navajo country with oral tradition is how well-preserved the ceremonial narratives are. The narratives are part of ceremonial repertoires—there are a couple of dozen repertoires—and these repertoires also include songs, prayers, paraphernalia, ritual procedures, sand paintings, and body painting. And the repertoires also include rules for combining these elements into a particular ceremonial performance for a particular purpose at a particular time and place. Parts of ceremonial narratives may be told during ceremonies, and each telling is tailored to the reason for the ceremony. But even so, the tellings are closely similar in each retelling. These ceremonial repertoires are big and elaborate and involve a lot of memorization of procedures and instruction on how to do the rituals, sand paintings, dance performances, and so forth. It takes years to learn these things. Well, each of these repertoires has a collection of narratives about its origin and development, and it is always emphasized that these have been handed down and you have to learn them just as told—not verbatim, the way songs and prayers are learned, but with the exact group of actors, events, and so forth. Those who learn more than one version are very careful that they tell one version or another but they don't combine those things and they don't put their own experience in the narrative. They may break out of narrative to comment or something like that, but that kind of personal experience or personal knowledge doesn't get into those narratives as they are handed down and there is a real concern about preserving the integrity of these narratives.

Many of the Navajo stories are only supposed to be told in the context of ceremonies in the winter time. When people like me do research, we haven't been taken out as a child and instructed. I'm more of an institutional link. I do my work kind of like you, Holly, do your work; we come into these communities as professionals rather than as integrated community members who will live in the community and carry on the traditions. But, with that as a caveat, let me give an example that may help to demonstrate the relationship between personal experience, ceremonial knowledge, and places out on the land.

I almost always work with one particular Navajo colleague. His name is Harris Francis. I guess it was about this time of year. We had talked to a ceremonialist for quite a while. This was a ceremonialist that Harris was fairly close to, and he had already told us a particular story. It is one of the ones I guess like the "Giant Footprints," one that kids tend to be told, not one of the more esoteric (and secret) ones. This was one that everyone knows, one you hear over and over again in different versions. This telling by the ceremonialist is the only one we have encountered that traced a route of travel on the ground for the heroes of the story. The ceremonialist had named a series of places and identified them for us in relationship to current landmarks and towns, and stuff like that. (That's the background.) Then, one time Harris and I were with this ceremonialist in view of one of those places, and the ceremonialist related how once in the past, he had driven down there and encountered these giant ants. In this case I can't say there was a clear moral lesson there, but I think in a way the point the ceremonialist was making to us is that this is not something we normally encounter and that this was a sacred zone. The unexpected happens in those kinds of places. That was his personal experience in this place that was named in this very ancient and well-known story. Most people can't even approximate where the place of that name is on the ground, but he could (because of what he had been told) and he was bearing witness to us that he had experienced something counterintuitive that validated what he had been taught about that area being a sacred zone. So when there is personal information like when you go to a place and someone alludes to an episode in one of these ceremonial stories, they will treat it the way the ceremonialist treated his experience with the ants, but those ants would never get into the age-old narrative of the heroes. The personal stuff is kept separate from the more traditional telling, but it's not unrelated; you just have to be careful how you structure your discourse to make those distinctions clear. You have to step out of the story if you want to apply a personal lesson. That's the way it is here, at least in my experience.

CUSACK-MCVEIGH: Interesting, because I can think of several situations where a teller will shift (in the same breath) from a well-known narrative to a more personal narrative describing an encounter, like the one you described with the giant ants, that is known to be out of the ordinary. And, as you said, it is a place marked by unexpected events. I have often wondered if that becomes more emphasized for the outside audience as another way to establish the value of the oral tradition, the old story that is the referent.

In one instance, an elder described an encounter with several otters and how they just weren't right; there were too many in one place. He knew right away he was at a place that was more significant than other places where one might encounter otters.

Another example where story, place, and social conditions come together is the shaman's grave at Hooper Bay. One teller alluded to this grave, explaining that in Yup'ik tradition, people were buried above ground. You can look out onto the tundra and still see these old graves today. On my first visit to Hooper Bay, I was told about the shaman's grave by a woman who had learned about it from her mother. Only once did she explicitly state to me that the shaman's grave was sinking (becoming level with the tundra) and that this was a sign of worsening conditions in her community and the larger world. She alluded to this place, I think, by way of getting me to recognize and take notice of the grave as a sign of conditions. Each time I returned to her village she would greet me by saying that "the shaman's grave is getting lower." This teller knows that I have enough cultural context to understand that this means, in her mind, things are much worse. This is also an example of how in Yup'ik discourse, some things are just too dangerous to mention directly. To speak explicitly of a painful event would be to invite it into one's own life. So the place of the shaman's grave provides this speaker a way to talk about things that cannot be otherwise spoken. And this works because I know the story and the place.

SCHNEIDER: In the Yup'ik examples you gave us, one's personal experiences in a way confirm the old stories, and the places reinforce the message.

CUSACK-MCVEIGH: Yes. The places and the stories are reminders of how to behave and the potential consequences of not following the rules of the society. The story of the "Giant Footprints" is, however, one of the strongest examples I have encountered in different contexts.

SCHNEIDER: Yes, that is one of the strengths of your paper: the attention to how the story is used. It seems clear that the "Giant Footprints" is really a cautionary tale and as such it is meant to be applied and told in the context of giving an indirect lesson, as opposed to telling someone directly that they are not acting right.

CUSACK-MCVEIGH: Well that is one of the things that it does. It is a cautionary tale particularly and primarily for those who are of the culture and are thought to be getting further and further from their cultural traditions. In many Native communities, that is a primary concern, because kids drift from their cultural values and social situations worsen. It also serves as a cautionary tale for those outside the culture who don't know the dangers and cultural ways.

KELLEY: Yeah, I think that is a concern around here too. There are some Navajo people who have been raised as Christians or are younger and are thought to not know anything about their culture. People are skeptical of them because all they have experienced is public school. Sometimes they are lumped into the same category as outsiders, and the attitude toward them is linked to the admonishment: "don't put aside your traditions. This is who you are, and you'll be nobody if you don't keep learning these things."

CUSACK-MCVEIGH: Yeah, these stories point out the real potential danger of letting the cultural traditions go. Places don't just remind people of story, places respond to human thought and action. Through stories of place, listeners can learn from the mistakes and naiveté of others. The place of the giant footprints remains significant in contemporary times because it speaks to people about the importance of following the words of their elders.

SCHNEIDER: It is appropriate that our discussion has brought us to the role of stories in establishing and maintaining the social order and the support systems of a culture. We have seen the power of story to operate in the personal sphere, as in your experiences, Holly, and through what you, Klara, have called the "received oral tradition." The linking of story to place in both ways anchors experience and memory to the landscape and is a strong form of reinforcement.

3

The St. Lawrence Island Famine and Epidemic, 1878–80

A Yupik Narrative in Cultural and Historical Context

Aron L. Crowell and
Estelle Oozevaseuk

Aron Crowell is an anthropologist and director of the Smithsonian Institution's Arctic Studies Center in Anchorage, Alaska. In his work at the Smithsonian he has created opportunities for Alaska Natives to share their cultural knowledge through exhibits and exploration of museum collections. The following essay was inspired by a trip to the Smithsonian with a group of Yupik elders from St. Lawrence Island. A magnificent gut skin parka led Estelle Oozevaseuk, his co-author, to retell her version of the St. Lawrence Island famine of 1878–80. The parka may date from that time and represents garments that were worn by the people who died. In her narration, the parka symbolizes their repentance for mistreating walrus and their preparation for passing to a promised land. Estelle's story challenges the "official" interpretation of what caused the famine and shifts the focus from the islanders' failure to hunt to acknowledgement of their transgression against animal beings. Documentary sources and oral tradition are presented to demonstrate how

each approach can add perspective to a tragic episode in the history of the Yupik people. This essay
was originally published in 2006 in *Arctic Anthropology*.

Introduction

The participation of Alaska Native elders in studies of museum collections and the development of exhibitions has created a new context for the recounting of oral traditions (Clifford 2004; Crowell
2004; Crowell, Steffian, and Pullar 2001; Fienup-Riordan 1996,
1998, 1999, 2005). In Native commentary, museum objects can
serve as anchor points for personal or collective histories—objects
as "signs," to use Susan Pearce's terminology (Pearce 1992:15–35).
Sometimes such objects are recognized as encompassing cultural
symbols, as when southwest Alaska Yup'ik leaders Paul John, Andy
Paukan, Wassilie Berlin, and Catherine Moore speak of being "in
the drum" as a metaphor for integral Yup'ik identity (Meade and
Fienup-Riordan 2005:111–17).

In 2001, a distinguished St. Lawrence Island Yupik elder, Estelle
Oozevaseuk (Penapak), joined other elders from the Bering
Strait region for five days of collections study at the Smithsonian
Institution's National Museum of the American Indian (NMAI) and
National Museum of Natural History (NMNH) in Washington, D.C.
The trip was one of a series organized by the Arctic Studies Center
and regional Alaska Native organizations to research the Alaskan
ethnology collections and lay the foundation for a collaborative
web catalog (http://alaska.si.edu) and large permanent exhibition
at the Anchorage Museum.[1] Mrs. Oozevaseuk, born at Gambell in
1920, is well known for her knowledge of St. Lawrence Island's cultural heritage. Her lifetime of community service at Gambell has
included work as a health aide, midwife, and teacher.

Among the objects that Mrs. Oozevaseuk discussed at the NMAI
was a *sanightaaq*, or ceremonial seal intestine parka (NMAI 123404).
The parka was donated to the museum in 1923 by San Francisco-
based fur trader Arnold Liebes, who purchased it on St. Lawrence
Island (Museum of the American Indian 1924:7). It is made of win-
ter-bleached intestines of bearded seal and decorated in a man's
style, with plumes and orange beak-plates of crested auklets. The
parka is further ornamented with baby walrus fur along the bottom
edge and with alder bark-dyed seal fur on the chest.

On the basis of its distinctive design and decoration, Mrs.
Oozevaseuk identified the *sanightaaq* as having originally belonged

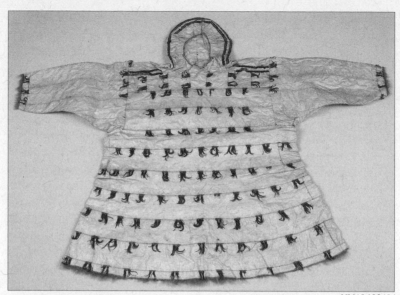

NMAI 123404

Sanightaaq, or ceremonial seal intestine parka, National Museum of the American Indian.

to a family from her clan, the Sanighmelnguut (also called Aymaramket), once living in the village of Kukulek on St. Lawrence Island. She added that the people of the village were well known for their beautiful clothing. In this connection, Mrs. Oozevaseuk narrated a traditional story, inherited from her grandfather Uwetelen (born 1865),[2] about the last days of the village and the mass death of nearly all its inhabitants. Through this account, Mrs. Oozevaseuk linked the *sanightaaq* to a pivotal event in St. Lawrence Island history. At the same time, her words limned the symbolic dimensions of the garment as a vessel of both Yupik and Christian meaning.

The loss of Kukulek occurred during the St. Lawrence Island famine and epidemic of 1878–80, during which more than 1,000 people (two-thirds or more of the population) may have perished (Ackerman 1976:38–39; Bockstoce 1986:136–41; Burgess 1974:28–32; Fortuine 1989:309–11; Krupnik 1994; Krupnik, Walenga, and Metcalf 2002). A recent analysis using archaeological and historical data (Mudar and Speaker 2003) projects an even greater loss of about 1,900 people out of a prefamine population of over 2,200. This disaster and its aftermath are described in a wide variety of sources, including Yupik oral tradition (H. Aningayou 1989; J. Aningayou 2002; Kava 1987:161–63; Kingeekuk

Estelle Oozevaseuk at the National Museum of Natural History, 2001.

1987a, 1987b; R. Silook 1976:62–63), contemporary written accounts by Euro-American witnesses (Elliott 1887:456–57; Hooper 1881:10–11, 1884:100–01; Muir 1917:108–09; Nelson 1899:269–70; Rosse 1883:20–21), and notes by others who gathered information from Yupik survivors and their descendants (Collins 1937:22–24, 2002:226; Doty 1900:187, 215–18; Geist 2002:235–38; Geist and Rainey 1936:10–11; Hughes 1960:11–13; Moore 1923:352–56).

Kukulek was also the site of massive archaeological excavations during 1931 to 1935, during which a large part of its historic ruins, artifacts, and human remains were removed (Geist and Rainey 1936). While this archaeological research today provides an additional source of information about life and death at the village, it was also a massive disturbance of the dead that was forbidden by local custom and belief (Healy 1889:12; Kingeekuk 1987b:115–16). Excavator Otto Geist shipped large numbers of human bones from the historic upper layer of the site to the Smithsonian Institution for study by physical anthropologist Aleš Hrdlička (Geist and Rainey 1936:48). These remains (estimated at 149 individuals) and others removed from the island in 1881 by Edward W. Nelson and Capt. Calvin Hooper (another 101 individuals) were held at the National Museum of Natural History (NMNH) until 1997, when they were repatriated to Bering Straits Regional Corporation under provisions of the National Museum of the American Indian Act (Mudar and Speaker 1997). Estelle Oozevaseuk served as a St. Lawrence Island representative during the Smithsonian repatriation process.

As discussed below, non-Yupik sources give various explanations for why hundreds perished in the winters of 1878–79 and/or 1879–80. Most accounts allege that an alcoholic "debauch" fueled by liquor from trading vessels caused the neglect of fall hunting, which led to famine and disease during a harsh winter of strong winds and poor hunting. The moralistic tone of these reports includes condemnation of the islanders' "improvidence" and "degradation" (Hooper 1881, 1884; Muir 1917:110; Nelson 1899:268–70). Yupik chronicles corroborate the occurrence of wind, bad ice conditions, severe hunger, and a swiftly fatal disease that devastated the island's population, while in most cases either placing little emphasis on alcohol or specifically denying that it caused the famine.

Estelle Oozevaseuk's retelling of Uwetelen's story presents an island-based view of the tragedy that diverges sharply from Western historical representations. The narrative interprets the famine within a framework of Yupik values and spiritual beliefs, reflecting, as oral historian William Schneider suggests, the common divergence between what is "reported" by outsiders and what is "told" within an interpretive cultural tradition (Schneider, personal communication, 2005). People of the village, it is said, cut skin from living walruses during a time of plenty, carelessly forgetting the importance of mutual caring and respect between animals and human beings. All that followed was a consequence of these actions. Directed by a spiritual leader, the people of the village dressed in beautiful clothing like the *sanightaaq* that inspired the story's telling, acknowledged their wrongdoing, received forgiveness, and died peacefully in their sleep, bound for a pure, white land as promised by their guide. Several other versions of this Kukulek story, or references to it (J. Aningayou 2002; Bogoras 1913:433–34; Doty 1900:218; Silook 1976:62–63) indicate that it has been part of the island's oral tradition since at least the 1890s.

An earlier recitation by Mrs. Oozevaseuk appears in a bilingual oral history collection published by the Bering Straits School District (Appasingok et al. 1987a,b; Oozevaseuk 1987), and she has told it many times to Yupik school children as an elder storyteller. She also presented it to a public audience at the National Museum of Natural History in Washington, D.C. during the 1982 opening of the exhibition *Inua: Spirit World of the Bering Sea Eskimo* (Fitzhugh and Kaplan 1982).

The contrasts between this narrative and other accounts of the 1878–80 tragedy, especially those authored by outsiders, are the focus of the present discussion. Perhaps its most striking feature is that Yupiget are held responsible for what occurred, not through improvidence but rather through a lapse in their regard for a spiritual code that sustains the life of all arctic hunting peoples. External and perhaps secondary "causes," whether weather, disease, or alcohol, are not adduced. Moreover, the story's imagery reflects a synthesis of Christianity with traditional Yupik belief. The challenge is to discern the present meanings and purposes of this living oral tradition. Indigenous narratives are often told *against* Western history, presenting representations of the past that are a foundation for contemporary cultural identity and autonomy (Crowell 2004; Friedman 1992). They are also told because they exemplify values and lessons for living that are relevant to the present lives and needs of Native listeners (Cruikshank 1998; Morrow and Schneider 1995).

The St. Lawrence Island Disaster Viewed from Multiple Perspectives

St. Lawrence Island has been home for almost 2,500 years to a Yupik population that subsists on the harvest of walruses, bowhead and gray whales, seals, fish, and seabirds (Collins 1937; Gerlach and Mason 1992; Hughes 1960, 1984). Of the island's two contemporary villages, Gambell, or Sivuqaq (population 649 in 2000) is by far the oldest, having been occupied for the entire human history of the island. Savoonga (population 643 in 2000) was founded in 1911–12. The Yupik language of Saint Lawrence Island is also spoken in villages on the near parts of the Chukotka mainland, some 40 miles to the west, with which the island has traded, married, and fought through the centuries. People of the island are affiliated to patrilineal clans (*ramket*), many of Siberian origin. Estelle Oozevaseuk's Aymaramket-Sanighmelnguut clan is from the village of Ungaziq (Old Chaplino or Indian Point) on Cape Chaplin. While many of this group migrated to Sivuqaq (Gambell) after 1880, others are said to have come earlier and to have resided at Kukulek at the time of the catastrophe (Krupnik 1994:57 and personal communication, 2005).

Western contact with the island, both direct and indirect, began with the Russian explorations of Bering (in 1728), Kobelev (in 1779), Billings (in 1791), Kotzebue (in 1816), and others (Burgess 1974). Intensive interaction with the American commercial whaling fleet occurred throughout the second half of the nineteenth century, when dozens of vessels stopped each year to exchange firearms, whaling guns, iron tools, cloth, hardtack, beads, and liquor for walrus ivory, baleen, furs, and clothing (Bockstoce 1986; Hughes 1960, 1984; Petroff 1882:10). Archaeological collections from Kukulek indicate the great extent to which the Yupiget had come to rely on imported iron tools by the late 1870s (Geist and Rainey 1936:133–34). In addition to bringing new implements, foods, alcohol, and diseases, the whaling fleet slaughtered massive numbers of the whale and walrus populations that were critical to the Native subsistence economy, almost certainly an underlying cause of the acute food crisis in 1878–80 (Bockstoce 1986:131–37; Jackson 1898:565). Cultural impacts of a different sort came with the establishment of a Presbyterian mission and school on the island in 1894, headed by Vene C. Gambell, after whom the village of Sivuqaq was renamed.

Estimates of St. Lawrence Island's pre-1878 population are uncertain, ranging as low as 300 to 400 (Dall 1870:537; Elliott 1887:546) and as high as 4,000 (Burgess 1974:63; Foote 1965), with 1,500 as the most commonly cited figure (Collins 1937:22–23; Ellanna 1983:69–77; Hooper 1884:100; Hughes 1960:12; Muir 1917:107–08; Teben'kov 1981 [1852]:36–38). Mudar and Speaker (2003) derive a population estimate of 2,274 from archaeological data, using counts and dimensions of winter house pits to calculate the populations of nineteenth century settlements (Collins 1937; Crowell 1984).

Teben'kov's charting survey in 1830–33 recorded five villages by name as well as a number of other smaller settlements (Teben'kov 1981 [1852], Map 19). Elliott recorded five principal villages in 1874, on the basis of a partial survey (Elliott 1887, end map). Based on historic sources, archaeological data, and villages named in oral histories (Apassingok, Walunga, and Tennant 1985, Apassingok et al.1987a,b; Krupnik, Walunga, and Metcalf 2002), there were at least ten large prefamine communities, including Sivuqaq, Kangii, Ivgaq, Kukulek, Kangighsak (Northeast Cape),[3] Punuk, Pukneliyuk, Kiyalighaq (Southeast Cape), Siknek, and Pugughileq (Southwest Cape), in addition to numerous smaller camps and warm season sites for fishing, hunting, and egg-gathering (Ackerman 1961;

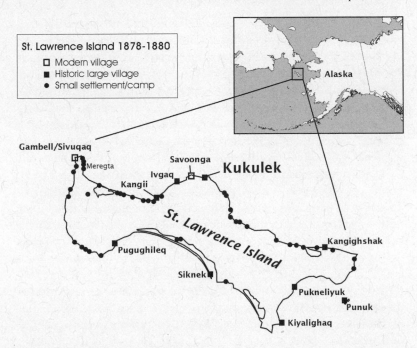

Historic villages and camps on St. Lawrence Island.

Crowell 1984). The first post-famine U.S. census in 1890 recorded 286 residents at Gambell (Porter 1893), not counting an additional 25 to 30 at Pugughileq (Krupnik 1994:56).

Historical Reports and Interpretations

Large-scale starvation brought about by sustained southerly winds and poor hunting for seals and walrus began in the winter of 1878, according to information gathered by trader J. J. Nye, who found no survivors at three of the four villages he visited in the fall of 1879 (Bailey 1880:26; Burgess 1974:29). Nye blamed alcohol brought by whaling ships for the failure of the islanders to lay in sufficient food supplies before the beginning of the hard winter. Another whaler, Ebenezer Nye, wrote to the New Bedford *Standard* in August 1879 that one third of the Native population south of St. Lawrence Bay, Chukotka (i.e., on both sides of Bering Strait) had died of starvation during the previous winter, including half of the people on St. Lawrence Island (Bockstoce 1986:137–38). He blamed the losses on severe weather and the depletion of walruses by the American commercial whaling fleet. In July 1879, A.

E. Nordenskiöld visited St. Lawrence Island and observed recent graves at Meregta (near Sivuqaq) but learned nothing about the disaster from survivors there, apparently for lack of a translator (Nordenskiöld 1881:250–56). In June 1880, Captain Calvin L. Hooper of the U.S. Revenue Steamer *Corwin* reported hundreds of dead at villages along the north shore of the island, including Kukulek[4] (Hooper 1881:10–11). His information, consistent with previous reports, was that these deaths occurred during the winter of 1878–79. Three hundred people at Sivuqaq had survived a second winter of bad hunting (1879–80), this time resulting from severe north winds, unbroken sea ice, and heavy snow. Relatively few died, but residents were forced to eat their dogs and the walrus hide covers of their boats and houses. It appeared that all other villages on the island had been abandoned. Hooper echoed J. J. Nye's opinion that drinking had played a major role in the two-year famine, and suggested that the islanders would soon be totally extinct if the liquor trade were not stopped. Henry Elliott also mentions that the winter of 1879–80 had been extremely severe, with ice that closed in around the island and kept the walrus herds far to the south (Elliott 1887:456).

The *Corwin* visited again the following summer (1881), this time with naturalist John Muir and Smithsonian naturalist-collector Edward W. Nelson on board. In late June, the vessel stopped briefly at Pugughileq (Southwest Cape), where there were many dead as well as two families of survivors (Hooper 1884:22–23). On July 3 the ship visited Sivuqaq and several abandoned settlements on the north shore of the island (Hooper 1884:33,100–01; Muir 1917:108–10; Nelson 1899:269–70). Both Nelson and Muir seem to have understood (in error) that the main loss of life had occurred in the winter of 1879–80. Their eyewitness descriptions of the abandoned villages are quite graphic. At one unnamed location, Nelson saw twenty-five deceased adults inside a single house, and others on the ground outside. The *Corwin* stopped at a much larger settlement where Nelson, Muir, Hooper, and I. C. Rosse, the ship surgeon, all went ashore. They found two hundred dead, many wrapped in reindeer skins and lying on the sleeping platforms of the semisubterranean winter houses, where they "met their fate with tranquil apathy," according to Muir. Inside one house about fifteen individuals had been placed in a pile. Other victims lay in the entryways to the houses, on the ground outside, or along the route to the community burial ground about one-half mile distant.[5]

It appeared that the initial effort to carry victims to the cemetery by sled had gradually been abandoned.

This village can be securely identified as Kukulek on the basis of archaeological data. Kukulek was the largest prefamine historic community on the north shore (with the possible exception of Sivuqaq), located on a high mound of older deposits that date back two millennia to the Old Bering Sea period (Crowell 1984:81–83). Its appearance is consistent with Rosse's observation that the location they visited "must have been a very old settlement, judging from the thousands of walrus skulls strewn in every direction and from the character of the kitchen-middens" (Rosse 1883:20). Muir reported that it had "about twelve houses" close to the beach, matching the eleven mapped at Kukulek by Geist and Rainey (1936:54). Archaeological descriptions of the people found at Kukulek—lying side by side or in piles on the sleeping platforms, collapsed on the ground outside, and along the route to the community burial hill—closely match the *Corwin* reports (Geist and Rainey 1936:55–81.)[6]

Captain Hooper recounted seeing an entire family of eight or nine who were found dead inside a summer house at the village.[7] Hooper thought the circumstances were strange, since a skin-walled summer house would not have been erected before the arrival of warmer weather and with it the opportunity to hunt seals in the open ice leads. He wrote,

> Believing they were doomed, they submitted quietly to what to them appeared inevitable, and daily growing weaker, stretched upon the ground and covering themselves with furs, waited for the end. In this position we found them lying as if asleep, their guns, bows, arrows, spears, and traps lying strewn on the ground. (Hooper 1884:100)

Reports by the 1881 *Corwin* group reflect differences of opinion about what had happened on the island. According to Nelson:

> Just before the time for the walrus to reach the island that season [which he dated Fall, 1879], the Eskimo obtained a supply of whisky from some vessels and began a prolonged debauch, which ended only when the supply was exhausted. When this occurred the annual migration of the walrus had passed, and the people were shut in for the winter by the ice. The result was that over two-thirds of the population died before spring. (Nelson 1899:269)

Nelson noted that some kind of disease had accompanied the famine. Hooper (1881, 1884) agreed that the tragedy originated in the abuse of alcohol, but along with Muir he doubted that hunger was the sole cause of death, because edible emergency foods such as walrus rawhide and other skins remained in some of the houses they visited (Hooper 1884:100–101; Muir 1917:109). In fact, he wrote, "the percentage of deaths appeared so extraordinary that I have at times thought the island must have been visited by an epidemic" (Hooper 1884:100). Rosse believed that disease was the most important cause for the loss of life and cited information from a whaling captain who had visited during the famine and observed that people were afflicted with "measles or black tongue"[8] (Rosse 1883:21). Unlike his compatriots, Rosse doubted that "intemperance" could have really initiated the disaster since, he argued, it was unlikely that the islanders could have obtained enough alcohol from any ship to last more than a few days.

Several general points may be made about these reports and conjectures by Euro-American observers, before considering Yupik memories and oral traditions about the events of 1878–80. The reliability of the information that Nye, Hooper, and others obtained on the island is open to question because of the brevity of their visits and difficulties of communication. For example, Uwetelen and others told Otto Geist in 1929 that no Yupik translator assisted Nelson in his inquiries (Geist 2002:238), and Rosse reported that the expedition's ability to communicate with local residents was "very imperfect" (1883:21). Negative racial stereotypes and cultural misunderstandings also came into play. Muir described the people of Sivuqaq as "simple and childlike" (Muir 1917:26), and Hooper depicted "Innuits" in general as filthy, savage, superstitious, dishonest, and lazy (Hooper 1884:99–113). In this vein he wrote that the people of St. Lawrence Island were vulnerable to famine because "they make no provision for the future, but depend on what they get from day to day." In actuality, Yupik subsistence activities from spring through fall (whaling, seal and walrus hunting, gathering seabirds and eggs, harvesting plant foods, etc.) are intensely focused on storing sufficient food for the winter (both today and in the past), although such efforts can fail in abnormal years.

The emphasis on alcohol in initiating the disaster, although supported by Yupik accounts for specific locations (see below), seems in general to be more a reflection of Euro-American prejudice or special interests than a logical or satisfactory explanation. Loss of human life during 1878–80 was so widespread—including substantial mortality in all the villages of St. Lawrence Island as well as simultaneous famine along the coast of Chukotka and at King Island—that it seems impossible to attribute it to the incidental procurement of liquor supplies at a few locations (Bockstoce 1986:138–141; Collins 1937:23–24; Doty 1900:217). Bockstoce (1986) suggests that Hooper and others connected with the U.S. Revenue Service may have exaggerated the alcohol problem to increase congressional alarm and funding for the service's arctic operations (1986:139). Additionally, walrus are normally available throughout the winter on St. Lawrence Island, not just during the fall migration (Ellanna 1983; Fay 1982), so that failure to obtain them had to be due to prolonged weather patterns or the impact of disease rather than to any temporary alcoholic incapacitation.

As shown by Igor Krupnik's analysis of post-1880 census data, more people survived at Kukulek, Kialighaq, Pugughileq, and other locations than historic reports would suggest (Krupnik 1994). Evacuees from these villages congregated at Sivuqaq, and clans identified with these historic settlements make up a large proportion of its current population. After the epidemic, Gambell's population was also bolstered by migration from Yupik villages in Chukotka (Burgess 1974:33; Geist and Rainey 1936:11; Porter 1893:8,165). Pugughileq, the only other village to survive the 1878–80 disaster, was inhabited until the 1930s.

Yupik Sources

Statements from Yupik sources confirm that the famine arrived with heavy fall winds from the south, southeast, and east that kept solid pack ice away from the island.[9] Winds and broken ice created impossible conditions for hunting walrus, either on foot or by boat, and strong currents caused the failure of seal netting at Sivuqaq (Collins 2002:226; Geist 2002:235–36; Giddings 1967:169; Hughes 1960:13). Paul Silook (Siluk, Estelle's father, born in 1893) told Henry Collins that this occurred in 1878 (or possibly a year earlier), corresponding with the chronology reported by J. J. Nye and Hooper. Geist's notes from discussions with Iqmaluwa, Uwetelen, and other elders in 1929 refer to the winter of 1879–80 as the primary period of famine (Geist 2002:235–38; see also Jimmie Ataayaghaq in Burgess 1974:68), preceded by a lesser crisis four years before that. Despite these inconsistencies in dating, all accounts agree that in the critical year solid ice did not form until January or February and that normal fall walrus hunting was impossible. According to Siluk, the bad ice and winds came on top of poor summer hunting, so that there were no accumulated food stores, and famine followed (Collins 2002:226).

At Sivuqaq, men sought desperately to hunt and some fell through thin ice and drowned or drifted away on broken floes (Geist 2002:236; Moore 1923:357). Sivuqaq men walked to Southwest Cape (Pugughileq) to trade whiskey for meat (see below) because seal netting had been successful there, and starving Kukulek people came to Gambell in search of food (H. Aningayou 1987:53–55; Geist 2002:236). One man (Ukaamangan) traveled to Sivuqaq from Punuk by sled at the beginning of winter, and had to stay there through the winter because people ate his dogs (Geist 2002:237; Moore 1923:357). The village of Pugughileq eventually ran out of food, and people there were reduced to eating old seal oil collected from lamps and the floors of empty meat cellars (H. Aningayou 1987:53–55).

While these testimonies clearly indicate widespread food short-ages, it appears that an unidentified epidemic disease (or several diseases), probably exacerbated by peoples' weakened condition, hit the island in early spring and was the primary vector of death. Jimmy Ataayaghaq (born 1878) recounted information to Francis Fay (in 1956 and 1961) that people at Kukulek and Kiyalighaq suf-fered from lack of food but that few actually died from hunger. In fact, hunting was good after the ice finally came in January and there was plenty of fresh meat, but the village was then struck with severe dysentery or diarrhea, from which many people quickly died (Burgess 1974:68). Survivors went to Sivuqaq, leaving behind full meat cellars. Geist's sources in 1929 also mention widespread deaths at Kukulek and Kiyalighaq from a disease that included severe diar-rhea, and which killed people even after they had obtained meat (Geist 2002:235). Akulki (b. 1844) told Riley Moore that people died at Sivuqaq (Gambell) from "acute indigestion" after eating the first walrus meat to become available in the spring, probably a ref-erence to the same fatal contagion (Moore 1923:357). Other Yupik accounts mention illness (combined with or following hunger) as a primary cause of mortality at Kukulek, Pugughileq, and Kiyalighaq (H. Aningayou 1987:53–55; J. Aningayou 2002:163; Kingeekuk 1987a:27; R. Silook 1976:63).

These accounts in general emphasize the rapid onset of the ill-ness, which killed people "in their sleep" and in large numbers, so that the dead could not be buried. The disposition of the bod-ies at the stricken villages, and discoveries of full meat cellars and edible skins (Collins 2002:226; Geist and Rainey 1936:57; Hooper

1884:100–101; Muir 1917:109) provide material confirmation of these Yupik accounts and of the primary role played by disease in the widespread devastation. Estelle Oozevaseuk herself commented about Kukulek that "some villagers from other parts of the island . . . tried to find out what caused them to die. Some thought about starvation. But when they check their meat caches most of them are full" (personal communication, October 28, 2005).

Additional support for this view is found in a remarkable narrative recorded by Waldemar Bogoras during brief fieldwork on the island in 1901 (Bogoras 1913:433–434). The teller was Ale'qat, described as "an Asiatic Eskimo." Ale'qat's "Creation of St. Lawrence Island" moves from the creation of the island to the story of a young man who is orphaned by starvation. Weak from hunger and covered with sores, he is saved when the Sea God mercifully provides fish, walrus meat, and seal blubber. The young man, tended by six women who are divine assistants of the Upper God, recovers and becomes a walrus-man who intercedes with another sky spirit (the "Sun Man") to bring an abundance of whales to feed the people. However, when the people of Kukulek kill this being by mistake he curses them, saying: "Such are you, and such shall be your fate. When you go to sea, you shall be drowned. When you stay ashore, you shall die of starvation. When you have food enough you shall be visited by the *tornaraks* [*tughneghaq*, shaman's familiar spirit, devil][10] of disease." In addition to its concurrence with specific events described in other narratives (e.g., the drowning of hunters, arrival of starvation, then illness), Ale'qat's narrative frames the disaster in cosmological and spiritual terms that resonate with the Oozevaseuk story.

There are several other specific references to Kukulek in recorded oral accounts. Two speakers mention that the famine was preceded by an earthquake, which caused stones to knock together on the beach, and the clay lamps to sway in the houses, frightening the people in the village (J. Aningayou 2002:163; Geist 2002:236). This was later viewed, perhaps, as a premonition of disaster. The same accounts say that after the epidemic some people were found at Kukulek in a summer *aagra*[11] lying peacefully together as if asleep, their heads on a wooden pillow, with water and meat in front of them (J. Aningayou 2002:164; Geist 2002:238), the scene apparently also described by Hooper (above). A rich man (Sigughwaaq), who bought many beads for his wife and even owned a set of brass armor, was found dead with his children and family inside a house that had been prepared for warm weather, further evidence that death struck in the spring after the food shortage had passed (Geist 2002:238).

While the majority of known Yupik sources either do not mention alcohol as a factor in the disaster or specifically deny that it played any role (Collins 1937:23–24; Hughes 1960:13), several do agree with historical reports that liquor was acquired before the famine, perhaps in substantial quantities. Elders told Geist that ships exchanged whiskey for baleen and walrus ivory during the spring and summer before the famine, and that one island man traded much of this supply (in barrels and bottles) to Kukulek and Kiyalighaq (Geist 2002:236–37). However, reports that heavy drinking was connected with the disaster seem to have come primarily from Pugughileq and Sivuqaq, the two villages that survived. Anagutaq (born 1866), a survivor at Pugughileq, said that walrus meat that had been stored for winter was traded away to men from Sivuqaq in exchange for liquor (H. Aningayou 1987:53–55). Aghtuqaayak (born 1877) said that people at Pugughileq were drinking when the ice came in and did not wish to hunt, thinking they had plenty of time to get food later on (Geist 2002:238). Akulki (born 1844) from Sivuqaq told Riley Moore that a large amount of whiskey was obtained from ships during the summer before the famine and that little hunting was done as a result, also mentioning one man who walked to Southwest Cape to trade liquor for food (Moore 1923:356–57). As argued above, the geographically widespread nature of the disaster and the documented impacts of bad weather and poor hunting conditions from summer through late winter of 1878 indicate that alcohol was a possible contributing factor at some locations, but unlikely as a primary or universal cause.

The Kukulek Narrative

This multisource review establishes that a sequence of circumstances and events—overall depletion of subsistence food resources by commercial whalers, sustained bad weather and hunting conditions, and an epidemic of one or more diseases that were highly virulent among the Yupik population (dysentery, measles, or other contagious diseases, perhaps influenza)—resulted in the dramatic and devastating loss of life on St. Lawrence Island in 1878–80. Ill-timed delivery of alcohol by trading ships may have exacerbated the situation in some villages, although this aspect was exaggerated in Euro-American accounts.

In the discussion so far, the historical actualities of people and events have been emphasized. The Kukulek narrative, on the other hand, seeks to provide an explanation of *why* such a tragedy could occur. While it draws on historical elements, perhaps most obviously the way that people at Kukulek and other villages seem to have died with calm resignation or in their sleep, its focus is on the ultimate cause of the tragedy rather than proximate causes or empirical facts.

Below is the complete narration, as presented by Estelle Oozevaseuk at the National Museum of the American Indian on September 10, 2001. She told it first in English and then agreed to our request to tell it a second time in her first language, St. Lawrence Island Yupik. The excellent transcription and translation are by St. Lawrence Island linguist, teacher, and historian Oovi (Vera) Kaneshiro (University of Alaska Anchorage), originally from Gambell.[12]

The People of Kukulek

(1) *Kukulegmiit, ayumiq, sivuneput.*
     (Kukulek people, many years ago, our ancestors.)
(2) *Elngaatall allaaghlluggaghtikat.*
     (They did something very arousing.)
(3) *Amyuqitiqeghllagluteng aatkiit—whaten legan—*
     (They acted very cruel—they did this—)
(4) *ukut aatkiit esghaghluki*
     (when I saw these, their clothing)
(5) *suumqaatkanka—iwhaani—uksuq pinighllaak,*
     (I'm thinking about them—and so—how nice their winter is,)
(6) *neqeteghllagyaqlegestun. Kiyaghteket elngaatall.*
     (much food should have been caught. They just lived like that.)
(7) *Nunavagllak pinghani atghaghluteng*
     (Whenever there were a lot of walrus on)
(8) *legan unguviita mangunameng*
     (the cake ice, men would cut chunks of edible)
(9) *ikulluteng, gaaghyaghqastun angkaan.*
     (outer skin even if the animal is alive, they cut one meal size.)
(10) *Amuqetiqeghllakat teghikusameng unguviita.*
     (They acted very cruel towards live animals.)
(11) *Taana esghaghu seghleghqellghat*
     (This incident of wrong doing, the cruel)
(12) *seghletun pillghat entaqun.*
     (thing they did had consequence.)
(13) *Seghleqellelgukaq esghapagtelghulghiikut.*
     (There is a being that watches over us.)

(14) *Taawa tawaten pighllagmi Kukulegmii uglaghllak yuuk.*
      (During this time there were a lot of people who were
      Kukulegmii.)

(15) *Yuggaq ataasiq esqaganlenguq akuzingigalngaq*
      (One little man who lived there somewhere in the village who
      didn't say much)

(16) *ukavaghpanlenguq elngatall qusevegngaghllalghii yuggaq*
      (who is considered a lovely person, he was a very humble little
      man)

(17) *pillguyugsigalnguq seghlequughngaatni*
      (who did not argue or try to be the key person,)

(18) *avelghaghaqegkangi*
      (even if they were not nice, he just ignored them)

(19) *liisimakeghngaaghmiki avelghaqiinaghaqegkangi.*
      (even if he knew that they disliked him he would ignore them.)

(20) *Tawaten sakaq, yuggaq aapghumangitughnguq*
      (Something happened, the little man did not tell what)

(21) *samatni naten liigikikumatneni.*
      (happened, how he came to understand what he had to do.)

(22) *Enkaam Kukulegmiit takwaaqluki aleghquqii.*
      (So he went to the Kukulek people and talked to them.)

(23) *Elngaatall aatkangllaatesqelluki,*
      (He put an emphasis on urging them to make clothing,)

(24) *whaten aarraasimeng.*
      (the kind that are dressy.)

(25) *Aatkiit igaghrakegteghllalghiit, satughllaget quunpeng.*
      (Their clothing had so much design and was very fanciful all the
      time.)

(26) *Kukulegmiit aatkaqeglleghuniiqegkanget, Qiighqami samani,*
      (The people of Kukulek were known to have fancy clothing on the
      island.)

(27) *almesiqegkangit. Ilangi repall*
      (they were always like that. Some of them)

(28) *sungaghmeng entaqun qughalkutiighlluteng ayuqaqelghiit.*
      (may have beads all around the clothing, probably like that.)

(29) *Taghnughhaqulluki aarraasimeng ulimatesqiit,*
      (He told them to even make fancy clothing for their children,)

(30) *pikegken naasqughhiitneng kanavek itegaghhiitnun.*
      (all the way from the head down to their feet.)

(31) *Taagken elngaatall aghnat kakitkaq,*
      (So then women sewed,)

(32) *kakiyupiglleghhiitlu entaqun esghaghhu,*
      (they were excellent sewers no doubt,)

(33) *sangita pimaaki.*
      (don't know why he had said that to them.)

(34) *Apeghiighyata taagken pimakangi,*
      (When they were all done he said to them,)

(35) *'Unaami piyukufsi avelghaqaghhaasi, navek pifqaafsi*
      ("Tomorrow, if you want to, refrain from going somewhere even if)

(36) *pinighllaghngaan esla.*
      (the weather is fine.)

(37) *Aliineghllugllagughngaan amsanaghllugllagughngaan.*
      (Even if it is very clear weather and calm weather.)

(38) *Aangghutkuminga uum kiyaghtaallemta esla pinighllequq."*
      (If my asking is granted by the way of life the weather will be fine.")

(39) *Unaami taghtughyalghiimeng legan amsanaghllugllak, meq*
      (The next day when they woke up it was so calm the water)

(40) *leganqun taghneghaghquuta, qagivleghaghhangunani*
      (was like a looking glass, not even a ripple of waves,)

(41) *imaghlluvleghaghhangunani. Elngaatall sumeghtaghaatkat,*
      (and no swells at all. So they put in this deep thought,)

(42) *Taawa yuggag temngi pingunghituq.'*
      ("So the little man is not just saying this.")

(43) *Aghuliitutkaq napigpenani yuuk nemetutkaq tamaana.*
      (People did not go anywhere, they stayed home.)

(44) *Taagken unugyagu esnamun—*
      (Then towards night, towards the beach—)

(45) *tawaten emta neqenghaghqumaghmeng pitkat.*
      (as usual they made so much food—they went.)

(46) *Quyatut elngaatall. Quyastekaqegkangi entagun qayughllak.*
      (They all felt very happy. He made them very happy supposedly.)

(47) *Kumaghtighllagluteng esnakun.*
      (They made a large fire at the beach.)

(48) *Leganqun laluramket bonfire-ngistun.*
      (Just like a white man's bonfire.)

(49) *Kumaghtighllakat unaghsimeng esnami.*
      (They made a big fire using wood at the beach.)

(50) *Neghuusimaghmeng.*
      (They were eating as well.)

(51) *Ataasikaghtaan ketfaghaqluteng esnemun tawavek pisqii tawaten.*
      (One by one he told them to come forward to the shore like that.)

(52) *'Seghleghqellesi apeghteghteki, qivghullesi sasi.*
      ("Tell the wrong things you have done, what you feel sorry about doing.)

(53) *Qivghukelleghsi seghletun pilleghpesinun.*
      (What you feel sorry for wrong things you have done.)

(54) *Apeghteghteki, ukmangightek elngaatall.*
      (Tell about them, cleanse yourself from them.)

(55) *Nuna uka tagiiquq qateghrakegllak, iqangilnguq avangilnguq.*
      (A place is coming that is very white, very clean and free of soil.)

(56) *Tawavek uugsaghqaaghtesqellusi pingwaamsi.'*
      (So you would be able to get on this place, I'm telling you.")

(57) *Naqamqun esgha tawaten qelellengumaat.*
      (So then they were given advice of what to do.)

(58) *Taana yuggaq akuzingigalnguq aangayugsigalnguq.*
      (That little man never said much, never acted big.)

(59) *Pillguyugsigalnguq sangigalnguq.*
      (He did not put on hot air, never did anything to be criticized for.)

(60) *Qallemsuggaq. Ugpeqegkaat.*
      ([He] was very quiet. They followed his advice.)

(61) *Esnevaghaqluteng. Leganqun apeghralghiistun pikat.*
      (People came forward. They just did like confessing.)

(62) *Sangwaa seghleghqelleghteng, seghletun pilleghteng*
      (Any wrong doing, anything they did that is wrong)

(63) *neqamikegqaghteng atightuqaat.*
      (that they remembered they told.)

(64) *Taaqenghata yuggaam aallgaqegkangi*
      (When they were done the little man would brush them off)

(65) *meghmun tawavek ukmangighniluki.*
      (towards the water, saying he cleanses them that way.)

(66) *Tunutestaqluki. Tawaten qamagtekaq,*
      (He made them turn around and brushed. He did that to everyone,)

(67) *iwerngaqun yugllak. Taawanguq whaten'nguq pikaqegkangi,*
      (all the many people. He had said to them,)

(68) *'Taghneghaghpesigun aaraaghlusi esghaghngaapesi whaa*
      ("Even if you see your reflection all dressed up like that have)

(69) *seghletun pillelgulghiisi. Ukmangighwaaghlusi esghiisqellusi*
      (wrong doing. It is for you to see how it is like to cleanse)

(70) *tawaten katam aarralleghpesistun, nunamun tawavek*
      (and dress nicely, you would be able to take a)

(71) *amllughyaghqaagusi. Ulimaaqamsi."*
      (a step over to that land (place). I prepared you.")

(72) *Taagken elngaatall quyatkat taaqluteng.*
      (Then they were happy when this was all finished.)

(73) *Enraqlunguq taam kingunganeng nenglum yuga*
      (Then after that all the people of that)

(74) *qamagtengngwaaghwaaghluni qavaghpagnikiit—*
      (subterranean dwelling place went into a deep sleep—)

(75) *ellngita tuqulaghaasata. Yupigestun*
      (that's the term they had used. When a person or group of people
       die in their sleep–)

(76) *tawateteftut qavameggneng tuqukat qavaghpagniluki.*
      (that was what happened to those people in their sleep.)

(77) *Qavaq, qavaq.*
      (Sleep, sleep.)

(78) *Qamagtengngwaaghluni imaa qaamna tuqulaghaatkaq nenglumi.*
      ("All the occupants of the house had died inside the building.)

(79) *Apeghiiqat entaqun apeghiighluteng.*
      (They were probably ready to go.)

(80) *Repall esghaghhu sumeghtaghaghaqelghiinga ilangani*
      (It really made me think, when I think about this sometimes,)

(81)   *entaqun quyastellghem saam kaatkaqegkangi.*
       (and think that they came to the conclusion of happiness.)
(82)   *Taawa nagneghunnaqaqegkegka sumeghtaghanemni, whaa.*
       (So I try to continue to tell about it when I think about it now.)
(83)   *Taananguuq whanga whaten kiyaghusiqa.*
       (That is what I like to tell about.)[13]

After concluding the story, Mrs. Oozevaseuk commented on one of its central points, saying,

> Because of my ancestor, I try to follow the pattern that he had, just like turning from bad living to good living. For their own future they [the people of Kukulek] did that. That may have been a blessing to them, that someone had compassion for them, after what they had done. So I told my grandchildren never to kill anything that is not edible.[14]

She concluded an earlier presentation of this story in the *Sivuqam Nangaghnegha* collection (very similar to the version here), by indicating another of its personal meanings:

> As I ponder this story, I am really amazed and now see comparisons. Thinking about them makes me thankful. I even tell our ministers, "I think that someday when the world ends we will see some of these Kukulek people who have found their salvation." In these events I see the mercy of God. The Eskimo people, like the white people, believed in God. They understood Him and honored Him in their own way. Even Eskimo people have their own standards of what is right and what is wrong. That is the way God made it to be. (Oozevaseuk 1987:89)

Meanings and Messages

Notably, the narrative starts at a point when walruses are plentiful, rather than scarce (lines 5–7), in an ideal time before the disaster. In an earlier telling of this story, Mrs. Oozevaseuk commented that life was so easy for the people of Kukulek that they were tempted to abuse things around them (Oozevaseuk 1987:87). In both versions, they cut and eat the raw skin from living walruses (lines 7–10), although Uwetelen said that they might have abused other kinds of animals (Oozevaseuk 1987:87) and according to the version narrated by Roger Silook (Saavla, born 1923, Estelle's brother), the people used their knives to cut *mangtak* (skin) from living whales (R. Silook 1976:62). These acts of cruelty to animals, and their fatal consequences for the people of the village, are dramatic and memorable features that appear even in shorter versions of the Kukulek story told by other narrators. For instance, James

Aningayou (Anengayuu, born 1878), reported in 1940:

> They had one time, I guess, a shortage of meat or something. Somebody [at Kukulek] strike a young male walrus, pull it right on top of the ice. Cut it up before it died. Kind of a cruelty, having a good time cutting that live walrus. That is the way they had their fun with it (*said in a disapproving tone*).[15] . . . And a short time afterward, same year maybe, something happened to them. Nobody will ever know exactly what happened to them, sickness or starving. (J. Aningayou 2002:163–64)

Doty also wrote that:

> An old woman who now resides at Gambell, having left one of those villages on the north shore during the fall preceding the fatality, or the previous one, asserts that the people of her village flayed a walrus alive and threw the suffering creature back again into the sea, in the hope that they would secure it in due time after it had gained a new skin. (Doty 1900:218)

The killing of a walrus being, who created the abundance of food enjoyed by the people of Kukulek but takes it away with his dying curse, is also the central theme of Ale'qat's 1901 account, as discussed above (Bogoras 1913:433–34).

The Kukulek narrative is told by Mrs. Oozevaseuk in the form of a Christian allegory. A good and humble man assumes the role of religious leader and leads the people out of temptation and sin through steps of spiritual preparation (lines 22–50), confession (lines 51–54), forgiveness and cleansing (lines 62–72), and then passage through death to a pure land (Heaven), where (as stated above) the Kukulek people find salvation. Punishment from God—the "being that watches over us"—is mixed with His compassion, and atonement brings joy, peace, and resignation. Putting on the white intestine parkas is an act of spiritual preparation for a journey through death to the world beyond (lines 68–71). The garments themselves seem to be a visual metaphor both for the heavenly land that is "very white, very clean, and free of soil" and for the souls from which all stains have been cleansed.

A strong Yupik spiritual dimension may also be discerned. Although God observes the Kukulek peoples' transgression from above, the sea mammals, in traditional Yupik belief, would be watching from below. At the center of Yupik and other arctic indigenous cosmologies (e.g., Bogoras 1904–09, Fienup-Riordan 1994; Hughes 1984; Jolles 2002; Lantis 1946; Nelson 1899; Rainey 1947; Spencer 1959) is the belief that mutual attentiveness and respect comprise the proper relationship between humans and animals. Hunting ceremonies, rituals, and observances, e.g., the wearing of clean, new clothing for hunting, the renewal of hunting gear and boat covers for each season, and the offer of fresh drinking water to newly killed sea mammals, are viewed as essential practices for hunting success and human survival. The consequences of the egregious disrespect shown at Kukulek—almost certainly, hunting failure and famine—would probably be an obvious point to Yupik listeners, even though not explicitly stated.

This view is partially illustrated in Mrs. Oozevaseuk's recounting of the story of Agnaga, a woman of the Uwaliit clan who went to live underwater with the seals, walruses, and whales.[16] In this tale the spirits of these creatures are human in both form and intelligence, and only certain traits, such as the seals' large eyes, reveal their animal nature. The walruses are large, stout men who keep their tusks in a side room of their underwater dwelling. Each day they put on their tusks and go out to seek the hunters, allowing themselves to be caught by those who have carefully made lines, floats, and hunting gear. Those who are struck by hunters with "dull" gear break the lines and return home with harpoon heads embedded in their bodies, which Agnaga cuts out using her *ulaaq* (woman's knife). When Agnaga journeys home to Sivuqaq on the back of a whale, she sees how the hunting boats appear to the animals from underwater. Some are light and clean, while others are black and cast dark shadows down to the bottom of the sea. The whale avoids the dirty boats but goes straight up to the cleanest, brightest one in order to be harpooned, even as Agnaga tries to hold him back. This story, told in Washington, D.C., two days after the Kukulek narrative, underlines that hunting is a collaborative effort in which animals participate voluntarily in response to human demonstrations of attention and respect.

An additional detail of the Agnaga story may be significant. As she cuts the harpoon heads from the wounded walruses, Agnaga steals bites of the animals' raw flesh. When she does so, the walruses cover their mouths, perceiving that she is eating the flesh of human beings, which is how they see themselves. The dual nature of the walrus-man (as well as his ability to influence the availability of game) is also explicit in Ale'qat's narrative, as previously discussed.

The role and actions of the spiritual leader in the Kukulek narrative—who is never named—seem to reflect a Yupik model of ideal behavior. He does not argue with the people or push himself forward but finds a way to both correct the community's bad behavior and to give them hope, without directly confronting or punishing. Significantly, he may have been a shaman, as Mrs. Oozevaseuk suggested in an earlier telling (Oozevaseuk 1987:87). Like a shaman he foresees the future and works to both heal the people and to restore balance with the animal world. When he brushes each person (lines 64–67) it is with a bird wing, a traditional gesture to remove sickness and evil influences (R. Silook 1976:7).[17]

The clothing that he tells the people to wear—especially the *sanightaaq*—was worn for traditional ceremonies of appeal to the animal spirits. This garment was decorated for men with auklet feathers and for women with tassels of fur from fetal seals. To make a *sanightaaq*, a woman first cleaned the intestines of bearded seals and then hung them outside to whiten in the cold and wind. She split the intestines and sewed them together with thread made of whale or reindeer sinew. Details of the design were different for each clan.[18] People wore these dress parkas for religious ceremonies such as Ateghaq, a spring sacrifice (*eghqwaaq*) held by each whaling crew to ask for good hunting; for Kamegtaaq, a thanksgiving that followed the hunting season; and for the ritual greeting that a whaling captain's wife gave to her husband's boat when it returned with a whale (Blassi 1985:217–223; Doty 1900:200; Hughes 1959, 1984:274–75; R. Silook 1976:18–20). The Maritime Chukchi wore them in ceremonies honoring the sea spirit Kere'tkun (Bogoras 1904–09:247). Perhaps in the Kukulek narrative when the people go to the beach and bend down to see their reflections in the still ocean water,[19] they are also showing themselves to the sea mammals below the surface, dressed in the beautiful garments they would always wear to offer supplication and to honor to the animals' ever-watchful spirits.

The spiritual synthesis that lies at the heart of the Kukulek narrative expresses Estelle Oozevaseuk's own view that Yupik traditional beliefs and morality prefigured what would be taught by the Presbyterian ministers who came to St. Lawrence Island in the aftermath of the disaster. About the sacrifices of food offered to a higher being by whaling captains in the spring *eghqwaaq*, she said "That's what the Eskimos believed long before they knew the Christian religion, they knew it. They knew about the Creator."[20] It may also reflect the changes in spiritual practice that the missionaries introduced to her family. Uwetelen, her grandfather, was a whaling captain and held the traditional spring sacrifices, but changed "his old custom," i.e., became Christian in 1929 or 1930 (P. Silook 2002:132). Her father Siluk, Uwetelen's son, was Christian from a young age, taught in the mission school, preached in the church, and rejected the old ceremonies.[21] To some extent, then, Mrs. Oozevaseuk's history of Kukulek may be her way of carrying forward the influence of both generations of familial teachers.

The story's basic themes—the necessity of treating all animals with respect, lest they cease to make themselves available to hunters; the responsibility of Yupik people for their own lives; the essential goodness of the Kukulegmiit, even in error; and the compatibility of Yupik and Christian beliefs—seem to be a lesson and a hopeful message for the communities of St. Lawrence Island. As the story continues to be told and retold, meaning has been created that extends beyond the actual events of 1878–80, meaning that is relevant to contemporary life. Anders Apassingok, Yupik lead editor of the Bering Straits School District oral history series in which Estelle Oozevaseuk's Kukulek narrative was first published, wrote that "the words in these pages are more than just facts or history. Behind the words is the heartbeat of the people. We want this heartbeat to live on in our children" (Apassingok, Walunga, and Tennant 1985:xvi).

Newly expressed in a museum context for a wide audience of web viewers and exhibition goers, the narrative can also be understood as an affirmation of Yupik pride and cultural identity against pejorative colonial portrayals of the island's culture and history (e.g., Hooper 1884, Muir 1917). Beyond this is the notable fact of the narrative's presentation at the Smithsonian Institution, where the physical remains and property of Kukulek's last residents were stored for more than a century. Estelle Oozevaseuk's retold tale may address, in a graceful and indirect way, the justice of her ancestors' return, and in a more general sense, the rightful reclamation of Yupik heritage and historical voice.

Acknowledgments

My appreciation first of all to Estelle Oozevaseuk for sharing her words and those of her grandfather and for applying her extensive knowledge of St. Lawrence Island history and culture to the interpretation of the collections housed at the Smithsonian. Sincere thanks as well to Oovi (Vera) Kaneshiro (University of Alaska Anchorage) for her fine translation of the Kukulek story and other materials from the Alaska Collections Project. Branson Tungiyan of Gambell, then director of Kawerak's Eskimo Heritage Program, helped to organize the Washington research and

contributed substantially from his knowledge of St. Lawrence Island traditions. Discussions in Washington, D.C., were facilitated by collections staff
of the National Museum of Natural History and National Museum of the
American Indian, with special thanks to Deborah Hull-Walski (NMNH)
and Pat Nietfeld (NMAI). Kristine McGee (NMAI) assisted with archival
research on the seal intestine parka. William Fitzhugh and Stephen Loring
(both with the Arctic Studies Center, NMNH) and Suzi Jones (Anchorage
Museum) lent their expertise to the collections dialogue. Dawn Biddison,
Alaska Collections Project researcher in Anchorage, coordinated and
contributed to multilingual translation and editing of the Washington
interviews.

This paper was first presented at the 2004 annual meeting of the Oral
History Association in Portland, Oregon, in a session organized by William
Schneider (curator of oral history, University of Alaska Fairbanks) and
Patricia Partnow (Alaska Native Heritage Center, Anchorage).

Igor Krupnik reviewed the manuscript and provided crucial points of
information from his St. Lawrence Island research. William Schneider and
Julie Hollowell also read the paper critically and offered useful commen-
tary. The excellent publication *Akuzilleput Igaqullghet: Our Words Put to Paper
/ Sourcebook in St. Lawrence Island Yupik Heritage and History*, compiled by
Igor Krupnik and Lars Krutak and edited by Krupnik, Willis Walunga, and
Vera Metcalf (2002) was an invaluable resource.

Funding for the present research and the Alaska Collections Project
was provided by the Smithsonian Institution, the Rasmuson Foundation,
the National Park Service (Shared Beringian Heritage Program), Museum
Loan Network (Massachusetts Institute of Technology), and Alaska
Humanities Forum.

Notes

1.   The Alaska Collections Project was organized by the Arctic Studies
      Center, Department of Anthropology, National Museum of Natural
      History, in cooperation with the Anchorage Museum; Kawerak,
      Inc.; Iñupiat Heritage Center; Yupiit Piciyaarait Cultural Center;
      Aleutian-Pribilof Islands Association; Tanana Chiefs Conference;
      Alutiiq Museum; and Sealaska Heritage Institute, with sponsorship
      by the Rasmuson Foundation, National Park Service, Smithsonian
      Institution, Museum Loan Network (MIT), and Alaska Humanities
      Forum. The Anchorage exhibition is scheduled to open in 2010.
2.   Yupik names and birth dates in this article are referenced to *Akuzilleput
      Igaqullghet / Our Words Put to Paper: Sourcebook in St. Lawrence Island
      Yupik Heritage and History* (Krupnik, Walunga, and Metcalf 2002).
3.   The small nineteenth-century Kangighsak Point or Kangighsak Camp
      archaeological site (Crowell 1984:98; Geist and Rainey 1936:7; Smith
      et al. 1978:48–50) is tentatively identified here as the village referred
      to as Northeast Cape in historic accounts (Doty 1900:187, 215–18)
      and visited by Hooper in 1880 (1881:10, his village "A," 10 miles west
      of Northeast Cape), where an estimated fifty people died in 1878–79.

Kingeekuk (1987a:23) refers to Qangeghsaq as one of the villages that existed when St. Lawrence Island had a large population.

4. His village "B" at "Cape Siepermo," a name derived from Teben'kov's chart.

5. Muir wrote that "Mr. Nelson went into this Golgotha with hearty enthusiasm," collecting over 100 human skulls along with bone armor, weapons, and utensils for shipment back to Washington (Muir 1917:110).

6. Nelson told Geist that Kukulek was "in all probability" one of the villages he visited in 1881 (Geist and Rainey 1936:85).

7. Hooper does not give the location for his observation, but virtually identical Yupik descriptions place this death scene at Kukulek (Aningayou 2002:164; Geist 2002:238).

8. Burgess suggests that "black tongue" may have been anemia, scarlet fever, or lack of vitamin B (avitaminosis) (Burgess 1974:56).

9. Burgess suggests that strong southerly winds and warm temperatures caused a lack of ice along the north shore in the fall and winter of 1878–79, whereas sustained north winds accompanied by heavy snow in 1879–80 packed solid ice along the north side of the island so that no open leads for hunting could be found.

10. From *A Dictionary of the St. Lawrence Island/ Siberian Yupik Eskimo Language* (Badten, Kaneshiro, and Oovi 1987).

11. The square, walrus-skin covered *aagra* was used in summer as a dwelling and in winter as the inner living chamber of the large, skin-covered Siberian style of dwelling called a *mangteghapik*.

12. Vera Kaneshiro is a member of the Pugughileghmii clan. Her willingness to provide a translation of Estelle Oozevaseuk's narration does not mean that Pugughileghmiit would tell the story in exactly the same way (Vera Kaneshiro, personal communication 2006.) In fact, a number of variants may exist among the island's fifteen clans. At least nine of these, including the Pugughileghmiit, are descended from the pre-1878 population, while others are postfamine immigrants from Siberia.

13. Alaska Collections Project Tape 12A:427–527, Arctic Studies Center, Anchorage.

14. Alaska Collections Project Tape 12A:527, Arctic Studies Center, Anchorage.

15. Comment in italics added by the story's recorder, anthropologist Dorothea Leighton.

16. Alaska Collections Project Tape 21A:77–318, Arctic Studies Center, Anchorage.

17. His use of a bird wing to brush the people is specified in Estelle Oozevaseuk's first telling of the story in English (Alaska Collections Project Tape 12A:309).

18. Alaska Collections Project Tape 12A:163 – 12B:375, Arctic Studies Center, Anchorage. Mrs. Oozevaseuk was taught these techniques by her grandmother.

19. This detail is specified in Oozevaseuk 1987:89.

20. Alaska Collections Project, Tape 16A:248, Arctic Studies Center, Anchorage.
21. Alaska Collections Project, Tape 16A:248, Arctic Studies Center, Anchorage.

References

Ackerman, Robert E. 1961. Archeological Investigations into the Prehistory of St. Lawrence Island. Ph.D. dissertation, Philadelphia: University of Pennsylvania.

———. 1976. *The Eskimo People of Savoonga*. Phoenix: Indian Tribal Series.

Aningayou, Hilda. 1987. "Starvation at Southwest Cape." In *Sivuqam Nangaghnegha: Siivanllemta Ungipaqellghat (Lore of St. Lawrence Island: Echoes of Our Eskimo Elders)*, Vol. 3, *Southwest Cape*. Anders Apassingok (Iyaaka), Willis Walunga (Kepelgu), Raymond Oozevaseuk (Awitaq), Jessie Uglowook (Ayuqliq), and Edward Tennant (Tengutkalek), eds., 52–63. Unalakleet: Bering Strait School District.

Aningayou, James 2002. "The Stories I Heard of Old Villages" (June 26, 1940). Excerpted from the Dorothea C. Leighton Collection, Archives of the University of Alaska Fairbanks, Folder "James Aningayou— Life Story," No. 3, Box 1. In *Akuzilleput Igaqullghet: Our Words Put to Paper: Sourcebook in St. Lawrence Island Yupik Heritage and History*. Igor Krupnik, Willis Walunga, and Vera Metcalf, eds., 163–65. Washington, D.C.: Arctic Studies Center, Smithsonian Institution.

Apassingok, Anders (Iyaaka), Willis Walunga (Kepelgu), and Edward Tennant (Tengutkalek), eds. 1985. *Sivuqam Nangaghnegha: Siivanllemta Ungipaqellghat (Lore of St. Lawrence Island: Echoes of our Eskimo Elders)*. Vol. 1, *Gambell*. Unalakleet: Bering Strait School District.

Apassingok, Anders (Iyaaka), Willis Walunga (Kepelgu), Raymond Oozevaseuk (Awitaq) and Edward Tennant (Tengutkalek), eds. 1987a. *Sivuqam Nangaghnegha: Siivanllemta Ungipaqellghat (Lore of St. Lawrence Island: Echoes of our Eskimo Elders)*. Vol. 2, *Savoonga*. Unalakleet: Bering Strait School District.

Apassingok, Anders (Iyaaka), Willis Walunga (Kepelgu), Raymond Oozevaseuk (Awitaq), Jessie Uglowook (Ayuqliq), and Edward Tennant (Tengutkalek), eds.1987b. *Sivuqam Nangaghnegha: Siivanllemta Ungipaqellghat (Lore of St. Lawrence Island: Echoes of our Eskimo Elders)*. Vol. 3, *Southwest Cape*. Unalakleet: Bering Strait School District.

Badten, Linda Womkon, Vera Oovi Kaneshiro, and Marie Oovi (compilers). 1987. *A Dictionary of the St. Lawrence Island / Siberian Yupik Eskimo Language*. Steven A. Jacobson, ed. Fairbanks: Alaska Native Language Center, University of Alaska Fairbanks.

Bailey, George W. 1880. *Report upon Alaska and its People*. U.S. Revenue Cutter Service. Washington, D.C.: Government Printing Office.

Blassi, Lincoln. 1985. The Whale Hunt. In *Sivuqam Nangaghnegha: Siivanllemta Ungipaqellghat (Lore of St. Lawrence Island: Echoes of our Eskimo Elders)*. Vol. 1, *Gambell*. Anders Apassingok (Iyaaka), Willis

Walunga (Kepelgu), and Edward Tennant (Tengutkalek), eds., 217–23. Unalakleet: Bering Strait School District.

Bockstoce, John R. 1986. *Whales, Ice, and Men: The History of Whaling in the Western Arctic.* Seattle: University of Washington Press.

Bogoras, Waldemar. 1904–9. The Chukchee. In *The Jesup North Pacific Expedition*, Vol. 7. Franz Boas, ed., 1–733. New York: E. J. Brill, Leiden and G. E. Stecher.

———. 1913. The Eskimo of Siberia. In *The Jesup North Pacific Expedition*, Vol. 38. Franz Boas, ed., 417–56. New York: E. J. Brill, Leiden, and G. E. Stechert.

Burgess, Stephen M. 1974. The St. Lawrence Islanders of the Northwest Cape: Patterns of Resource Utilization. Ph.D. dissertation, Department of Environmental Sciences, Fairbanks: University of Alaska Fairbanks.

Clifford, James 2004. Looking Several Ways: Anthropology and Native Heritage in Alaska. *Current Anthropology* 45(1):5–30.

Collins, Henry. 1937. *Archeology of St. Lawrence Island, Alaska.* Washington, D.C.: Government Printing Office.

———. 2002. St. Lawrence Island "Old Stories." Excerpts from St. Lawrence Island field notes of 1928–30, National Anthropological Archives. In *Akuzilleput Igaqullghet: Our Words Put to Paper: Sourcebook in St. Lawrence Island Yupik Heritage and History.* Igor Krupnik, Willis Walunga, and Vera Metcalf, eds., 226–34. Washington, D.C.: Arctic Studies Center, Smithsonian Institution.

Crowell, Aron L. 1984. Archaeological Survey and Site Condition Assessment of St. Lawrence Island, Alaska. Final report submitted to the Smithsonian Institution, Alaska Office of History and Archaeology (Anchorage), and Sivuqaq, Inc. (Gambell).

———. 2004. Terms of Engagement: The Collaborative Representation of Alutiiq Identity. *Ètudes/Inuit/Studies* 28(1):9–35.

Crowell, Aron L., Amy F. Steffian, and Gordon L. Pullar (eds.). 2001. *Looking Both Ways: Heritage and Identity of the Alutiiq People.* Fairbanks: University of Alaska Press.

Cruikshank, Julie. 1998. *The Social Life of Stories: Narrative and Knowledge in the Yukon Territory.* Lincoln: University of Nebraska Press.

Dall, William H. 1870. *Alaska and its Resources.* Boston: Lee and Shepard.

Doty, William F. 1900. The Eskimo on St. Lawrence Island, Alaska. In *Ninth Annual Report on Introduction of Domestic Reindeer in Alaska, 1899.* Sheldon Jackson, ed., 186–223. Washington, D.C.: Government Printing Office.

Ellanna, Linda J. 1983. Bering Strait Insular Eskimo: A Diachronic Study of Economy and Population Structure. Technical Paper No. 77. Juneau: Division of Subsistence, Alaska Department of Fish and Game.

Elliott, Henry W. 1887. *Our Arctic Province: Alaska and the Seal Islands.* New York: Charles Scribner's Sons.

Fay, F. H. 1982. *Ecology and Biology of the Pacific Walrus*, Odobenus rosmarus diivergens *Illiger.* Washington: U.S. Department of the Interior, Fish and Wildlife Service.

Fienup-Riordan, Ann. 1994. *Boundaries and Passages: Rule and Ritual in Yup'ik Eskimo Oral Tradition.* Norman: University of Oklahoma Press.

———. 1996. *The Living Tradition of Yup'ik Masks / Agayuliyararput: Our Way of Making Prayer.* Seattle: University of Washington Press.

———. 1998. Yup'ik Elders in Museums: Fieldwork Turned on its Head. *Arctic Anthropology* 35(2):49–58.

———. 1999. Collaboration on Display: A Yup'ik Eskimo Exhibit at Three National Museums. *American Anthropologist* 101(2):339–58.

———. 2005. *Yup'ik Elders at the Ethnologisches Museum Berlin: Fieldwork Turned on its Head.* Seattle: University of Washington Press.

Fitzhugh, William W., and Susan A. Kaplan. 1982. *Inua: Spirit World of the Bering Sea Eskimo.* Washington, D.C.: Smithsonian Institution Press.

Foote, Don C. 1965. Exploration and Resource Utilization in Northwestern Arctic Alaska Before 1855. Ph.D. dissertation. Montreal: Geography Department, McGill University.

Fortuine, Robert. 1989. *Chills and Fever: Health and Disease in the Early History of Alaska.* Fairbanks: University of Alaska Press.

Friedman, Jonathan. 1992. The Past in the Future: History and the Politics of Identity. *American Anthropologist* 94(4):837–59.

Geist, Otto W. 2002. "Notes Regarding the Famine and Epidemics on St. Lawrence Island During the Winter of 1879–80" (March 29, 1929). Otto W. Geist Collection, Box 3, Folder 68, Rasmuson Library Archives, University of Alaska Fairbanks. In *Akuzilleput Igaqullghet: Our Words Put to Paper: Sourcebook in St. Lawrence Island Yupik Heritage and History.* Igor Krupnik, Willis Walunga, and Vera Metcalf, eds., 235–38. Washington, D.C.: Arctic Studies Center, Smithsonian Institution.

Geist, Otto W., and Froelich G. Rainey. 1936. *Archaeological Excavation at Kukulik, St. Lawrence Island, Alaska: Preliminary Report.* Miscellaneous Publications, University of Alaska, Vol. II. Washington, D.C.: Government Printing Office.

Gerlach, Craig, and Owen K. Mason. 1992. Calibrated Radiocarbon Dates and Cultural Interaction in the Western Arctic. *Arctic Anthropology* 29(1):54–81.

Giddings, J. Louis. 1967. *Ancient Men of the Arctic.* New York: Alfred A. Knopf.

Healy, Capt. M. A. 1889. *Report of the Cruise of the Revenue Marine Steamer Corwin in the Arctic Ocean in the Year 1884.* Washington, D.C.: Government Printing Office.

Hooper, Calvin L. 1881. *Report on the Cruise of the U.S. Revenue Steamer Corwin in the Arctic Ocean, November 1, 1880.* Washington, D.C.: Government Printing Office.

———. 1884. *Report of the U. S. Revenue Steamer Thomas Corwin in the Arctic Ocean, 1881.* Washington, D.C.: Government Printing Office.

Hughes, Charles C. 1959. Translation (from the Russian) of I. K. Voblov's "Eskimo Ceremonies." *Anthropological Papers of the University of Alaska* 7(2):71–90.

————. 1960. *An Eskimo Village in the Modern World.* With the collaboration of Jane M. Hughes. Ithaca: Cornell University Press.

————. 1984. Saint Lawrence Island Eskimo. In *Handbook of North American Indians*, Vol. 5, *Arctic.* David Damas, ed.. William C. Sturtevant, general editor. Washington, D.C.: Smithsonian Institution Press. 262–77.

Jackson, Sheldon. 1898. Introduction of Domestic Reindeer into Alaska. In *Seal and Salmon Fisheries and General Resources of Alaska 1898*, Vol. III, 565–74. Washington, D.C.: Government Printing Office.

Jolles, Carol Zane. 2002. *Faith, Food, and Family in a Yupik Whaling Community.* Seattle: University of Washington Press.

Kava, Bobby. 1987. My Growing Up Years. In *Sivuqam Nangaghnegha: Siivanllemta Ungipaqellghat (Lore of St. Lawrence Island: Echoes of our Eskimo Elders)*, Vol. 2, *Savoonga.* Anders Apassingok (Iyaaka), Willis Walunga (Kepelgu), Raymond Oozevaseuk (Awitaq), and Edward Tennant (Tengutkalek), eds., 153–79. Unalakleet: Bering Strait School District.

Kingeekuk, Ronald. 1987a. Early Island History. In *Sivuqam Nangaghnegha: Siivanllemta* Ungipaqellghat *(Lore of St. Lawrence Island: Echoes of our Eskimo Elders)*, Vol. 2, *Savoonga.* Anders Apassingok (Iyaaka), Willis Walunga (Kepelgu), Raymond Oozevaseuk (Awitaq), and Edward Tennant (Tengutkalek), eds., 23–31. Unalakleet: Bering Strait School District.

————. 1987b. The Men Who Drifted Off on the Ice. In *Sivuqam Nangaghnegha: Siivanllemta Ungipaqellghat (Lore of St. Lawrence Island: Echoes of our Eskimo Elders)*, Vol. 2, *Savoonga.* Anders Apassingok (Iyaaka), Willis Walunga (Kepelgu), Raymond Oozevaseuk (Awitaq), and Edward Tennant (Tengutkalek), eds., 113–29. Unalakleet: Bering Strait School District.

Krupnik, Igor. 1994. "Siberians" in Alaska: The Siberian Eskimo Contribution to Alaskan Population Recoveries, 1880–1940. *Études/Inuit/Studies* 18(1–2):49–80.

Krupnik, Igor, Willis Walunga, and Vera Metcalf (eds.). 2002. *Akuzilleput Igaqullghet: Our Words Put to Paper: Sourcebook in St. Lawrence Island Yupik Heritage and History.* Washington, D.C.: Arctic Studies Center, Smithsonian Institution.

Lantis, Margaret. 1946. *The Social Culture of the Nunivak Eskimo.* Transactions of the American Philosophical Society n.s. Vol. 35, pt. 3, p. 153, 156–316.

Meade, Marie (trans.), and Ann Fienup-Riordan (ed.). 2005. *Ciuliamta Akliut / Things of Our Ancestors: Yup'ik Elders Explore the Jacobsen Collection at the Ethnologisches Museum Berlin.* Seattle: University of Washington Press.

Moore, Riley D. 1923. Social Life of the Eskimo of St. Lawrence Island. *American Anthropologist* 25(3):339–75.

Morrow, Phyllis, and William Schneider. 1995. *When Our Words Return: Writing, Hearing, and Remembering Oral Traditions of Alaska and the Yukon.* Logan: Utah State University Press.

Mudar, Karen, and Stuart Speaker. 1997. Inventory and Assessment of Human Remains from St. Lawrence Island, Alaska in the National Museum of Natural History. Washington, D.C.: Repatriation Office, Department of Anthropology, National Museum of Natural History.

————. 2003. Natural Catastrophes in Arctic Populations: The 1878–1880 Famine on St. Lawrence Island, Alaska. *Journal of Anthropological Archaeology.* 22:75–104.

Muir, John. 1917. *The Cruise of the* Corwin: *Journal of the Arctic Expedition in 1881 in Search of De Long and the Jeanette.* William Frederic Badé, ed. Boston and New York: Houghton Mifflin.

Museum of the American Indian (National Museum of the American Indian). 1924. Annual Report for the Period from April 1, 1923, to April 1, 1924, of the Board of Trustees of the Museum of the American Indian, Heye Foundation, to George C. Heye, Grantor. New York.

Nelson, Edward William. 1899. The Eskimo about Bering Strait. In *Eighteenth Annual Report of the Bureau of American Ethnology 1896–1897.* 3–518. Washington, D.C.: Government Printing Office.

Nordenskiöld, A. E. 1881. *The Voyage of the Vega Round Asia and Europe.* Translated by Alexander Leslie. 2 vols. London: Macmillan and Co.

Oozevaseuk, Estelle. 1987. The People of Kukulek. In *Sivuqam Nangaghnegha: Siivanllemta Ungipaqellghat (Lore of St. Lawrence Island: Echoes of our Eskimo Elders),* Vol. 3, *Southwest Cape.* Anders Apassingok (Iyaaka), Willis Walunga (Kepelgu), Raymond Oozevaseuk (Awitaq), Jessie Uglowook (Ayuqliq), and Edward Tennant (Tengutkalek), eds., 86–89. Unalakleet: Bering Strait School District.

Pearce, Susan M. 1992. *Museums, Objects, and Collections: A Cultural Study.* Washington, D.C.: Smithsonian Institution Press.

Petroff, Ivan. 1882. Report on the Population, Industries, and Resources of Alaska. In *Tenth Census of the United States 1880, Alaska.* Washington, D.C.: Department of the Interior, Census Office.

Porter, Robert P. 1893. *Report on Population and Resources of Alaska at the Eleventh Census, 1890.* Washington, D.C.: U.S. Government Printing Office.

Rainey, Froelich G. 1947. The Whale Hunters of Tigara. *Anthropological Papers of the American Museum of Natural History* 41, pt. 2: 231–32, 235–83.

Rosse, Irving C. 1883. Medical and Anthropological Notes on Alaska. In *Cruise of the Revenue-Steamer* Corwin *in Alaska and the N. W. Arctic Ocean in 1881, Notes and Memoranda: Medical and Anthropological: Botanical: Ornithological,* 9–43. Washington, D.C.: Government Printing Office.

Silook, Paul. 2002. "My Early Memories." Excerpted from the Dorothea C. Leighton Collection, Archives of the University of Alaska, Fairbanks, Folder "Paul Silook—Autobiography," No. 66, Box 3. In *Akuzilleput Igaqullghet: Our Words Put to Paper: Sourcebook in St. Lawrence Island Yupik Heritage and History.* Igor Krupnik, Willis Walunga, and Vera Metcalf, eds., 130–38. Washington, D.C. Arctic Studies Center, Smithsonian Institution.

Silook, Roger S. 1976. *Seevookuk: Stories the Old People Told on St. Lawrence Island.* Anchorage: Alaska Publishing Company.

Smith, George S., Zorro A. Bradley, Ronald E. Kreher, and Terry P. Dickey. 1978. The Kialegak Site, St. Lawrence Island, Alaska. Occasional Paper No. 10, *Anthropology and Historic Preservation.* Fairbanks: Cooperative Park Studies Unit, University of Alaska Fairbanks.

Spencer, Robert F. 1959. *The North Alaskan Eskimo: A Study in Ecology and Society.* Smithsonian Institution, Bureau of American Ethnology Bulletin 171. Washington, D.C.: Smithsonian Institution Press.

Teben'kov, M. D. 1981 [1852]. *Atlas of the Northwest Coasts of America, from Bering Strait to Cape Corrientes and the Aleutian Islands.* Originally published 1852. Translated and edited by Richard A. Pierce. Kingston, Ontario: Limestone Press.

The St. Lawrence Island Famine and Epidemic, 1878–80

A Conversation with Aron L. Crowell and
James Clifford

In the following discussion, James Clifford helps us to understand Estelle Oozevaseuk's story in a broader framework. He sees it as part of a movement of indigenous peoples all over the world who are seeking ways to express their own stories, to contribute to history making, and to challenge the narrowness of the "official record." Crowell and Clifford explore how Estelle Oozevaseuk's narration imparts a message for the present. Similarly, they recognize the Yupik parka at the Smithsonian as more than a material vestige of the past; instead, it is a vehicle of expression, pregnant with story.

CLIFFORD: I see Aron's text falling into two distinct but interconnected moments. The first is an exercise in critical historical work that would be appreciated by any historian influenced by ethnohistory in the style of Jan Vansina. Here the idea is that by using both written and oral sources, according them equal weight and critical analysis, you try to make the best interpretation, the most balanced guess about what really happened. You draw on every kind of source to produce judgments of an historical realist sort.

But then, there is the other part of Aron's essay. He shows us that Estelle's narrative refers not only to things widely recognizable as historically real but also to what we might call ultimate meanings—truths of ethics and spirituality. This is not about how historians

James Clifford is professor of history of consciousness at the University of California Santa Cruz. Among his interests are how local and indigenous groups respond to national and international forces and the role of museums and festivals as settings for cultural expression. Some of his best-known publications include *Writing Culture: The Poetics and Politics of Ethnography* (1986), edited with George E. Marcus; the *Predicament of Culture: Twentieth Century Ethnography, Literature, and Art* (1988); and *Routes: Travel and Translation in the Late Twentieth Century* (1997).

typically ask "why" something happened. Rather, it concerns the allegorical dimensions that every story produces in its listeners in the present context of its telling. Stories are never limited to just telling the facts, what really happened, once, in historical time. People will always add levels of significance, and Estelle is expressing quite specific meanings that, as Aron shows, combine Christian elements with traditional knowledge of various sorts. What interests me is the way Estelle's story adds an overlapping, not an opposed, ontology to the historical record. Her listeners recognize the full history she is retelling, both a traumatic series of real events in the past and an ethical vision, an allegory that resonates in very direct and important ways in their ongoing lives.

SCHNEIDER: Is that because stories are told in the present, and the present has its own particular considerations and questions that the story can address?

CLIFFORD: Yes. Where I begin in Aron's piece is the final words. He talks about Estelle reclaiming Yupik heritage in the context of a museum, with repatriation in the air, since the islanders are at the Smithsonian to reconnect with their cultural objects. Aron says Estelle is reclaiming "Yupik heritage and historical voice," and it is *historical voice* that I would underline. Heritage is more than just recollection, reclaiming a lost or silenced collective reality. It's creative, changing. Heritage as historical *voice* is performative: there's always an "I" and a "you," a specific relation. The message and its reception exist essentially in the present moment: Estelle and her fellow villagers at the Smithsonian, and us trying to understand what they were saying—to each other, and to us. Who is being addressed, and what do they hear and what don't they hear? There's something coming across in every story, but something missed. So *voice* to me suggests performance, articulation, and translation. These are the terms—all stressing partial, contingent connection—that I keep coming back to in thinking about cultural process and transformation. And *historical* suggests something more than just folklore or a local belief system. The historically real, here, is an open-ended, relational process.

CROWELL: It also seems to me that historical voice—the way history is told—is an expression and a foundation of cultural identity. For example, Jonathan Friedman in his essay "The Past in the Future: History and the Politics of Identity" emphasizes that history and identity are constructed in relation to each other. I especially appreciate Anders Apassingok's introduction to the collected oral traditions of St. Lawrence Island, in which he says that "the words on these pages are more than facts and history. Behind the words is the heartbeat of the people." In this sense, the Kukulek narrative is a mirror of collective Yupik identity, a reflection on "who we are" and what happens when fundamental values of the culture are transgressed. Estelle Oozevaseuk is carrying the message of this generations-old story into the present.

At the same time, it is important to remember that this particular version evolved within a specific family and clan context. Yupik linguist Vera Kaneshiro, who translated the narrative for publication, said that the famine and events at Kukulek are recounted somewhat differently by people of other clans. The story thus has a specificity to the narrator and her family, and we should keep in mind that other contemporary perspectives may exist regarding the meaning of this watershed event in St. Lawrence Island history. This variation is not something that I have had the opportunity to explore.

We can also see, as Jim mentioned, how new meanings are added over time. The Bogoras version of the Kukulek story, recorded in 1901, is more closely aligned with traditional Yupik cosmology, without any overlay of Christian belief. The Presbyterian mission had been established on the island only a few years earlier, in 1894, and the way that Ale'qat told the story to Bogoras is probably close to the way that people originally "constructed" the events of 1878–80. The redemptive Christian narrative was later melded with the original story, adding a new layer of meaning without erasing the old. Today, the significance of Estelle's narrative may lie especially in its implications for Yupik identity, self sufficiency, and self regard. In part this is no doubt a reaction to pejorative accounts of the disaster that have been given by Western writers.

There is an interesting illustration of how the history of the "famine" lives on in peoples' minds. In 2005, Gambell resident Douglas Henry found an old underground meat cache buried about eight feet down in the frozen soil of the Siqlugaghyaget archaeological site, adjacent to the modern village. Blubber from the cache was eventually radiocarbon dated to about 1,100 years before present, but before this result was known some residents of Gambell suggested that the meat remained from 1878, proof that people had not failed to provide themselves with meat and were not to blame for the disaster.

CLIFFORD: A Native counter-history or critical genealogy? I have been thinking recently about the range of historical idioms, the kinds of stories that various indigenous movements are telling these days. There often seems to be an element of "setting the record straight," a way of putting the *colonial* moment—and that can be a very long and unfinished moment—in its place, recontextualizing it within a longer indigenous historical temporality. Sometimes that temporality takes a cyclical form. You know there's a quote from an Alutiiq elder, Barbara Shangin, that has made me stop and think a lot about historical voice. She says, in effect: "Ever since the Russians came it has been one big spell of storms and bad weather. . . . But this too will pass." Her metaphor suggests a kind of cyclicality but, of course, weather is both the same and never the same each time around. We never come full circle to a previous state. So this indigenous counter-discourse is always about more than correcting the colonial record. Like Estelle's story, it's a matter of producing some bigger, deeper, open-ended story about indigenous continuity, and enduring ethical purpose, through these terrible struggles and transformations. In indigenous historical narratives—which often avoid stark before/after ruptures and zero-sum transitions—religious conversion is not a loss but an addition, or rather a selective rearticulation and translation. We didn't lose who we were when we became Christians; we added something important without letting go. Identity is a process. I see something of this building of narratives of continuity and overcoming in Estelle's historical voice.

CROWELL: I believe that is true for St. Lawrence Island. And as part of that, there's a great deal of pride and a strong commitment to independence and autonomy. During implementation of the Alaska Native Claims Settlement Act, the islanders let go of any cash settlement they might have received in exchange for full title to the whole island. They didn't want any part of their land to go to outside interests. It is an example of their efforts to preserve the integrity of the culture.

CLIFFORD: Aron, I want to hear just a little bit more about the object, the parka, that provoked this retelling. I'm really curious about the power of clothing—and I don't mean clothing in any kind of narrow Western way. How does something like this parka manifest the self through social (including interspecies) cosmological relations?

CROWELL: When Estelle saw the parka at the Smithsonian, she identified the design with her clan and it prompted her to tell the story. This type of garment was associated with sacred events, such as the arrival and welcome of a whale that had been killed. During the traditional hunting ceremonies, people would nearly always wear these decorated parkas, which were made from parts of seals, walruses, whales, and birds. Their beauty was an expression of respect toward these nonhuman beings, which give themselves to sustain the human community. Of all the things in museum collections, clothing is often the richest source of thought, recollection, and stories because it ties into so many social and spiritual dimensions.

CLIFFORD: The parka in this story is a beautiful example of that point. Museum objects are not what really matters, in a sense—what matters are the stories that are associated with the object. And the stories may be specific to particular clans or families who have rights to tell them. Provoked by the object, the stories are retold, always in a new context, to make us look both ways, to reach back to something and to go forward. Ann Fienup-Riordan's recent accounts of her visits with Yup'ik elders to the collections of various museums in Germany shows this in detail. And Julie Cruikshank's work has also been very important to me in thinking about the ongoing life of stories and the attitude of elders who see them, not primarily as something to preserve, but as a way of "making history" now. I think the whole repatriation process, whether it is about things actually coming back to live in tribal settings or whether it is about tribal people visiting and reclaiming links with objects held in urban museums, the whole process represents an enormous remaking and retelling that is going on around these objects and stories. And the word "object" just doesn't work anymore.

CROWELL: I've often had the experience of seeing these items in their drawers, bereft of any of this knowledge. And I realize that each one could be connected to a whole system of understandings and associations. The signs embodied by clothing and other types of material culture can't be understood until they are rejoined with the universe of understanding that elders can bring forth in their descriptions and accounts.

I also had the privilege of working with Estelle's late brother, Roger Silook, on a teaching project at the Anchorage Museum. He and his daughter, ivory artist Susie Silook, were invited as guest curators for a "one-day exhibit" exercise that we organized for a tribal museum training course. The pieces for the show came from the museum's collection of St. Lawrence Island archaeological artifacts. In the morning, Roger stood before the group, held the pieces up one by one, and talked about them in just a brilliant way. He brought out stories about each one and how it might have been used. During lunch, Ann Fienup-Riordan and I condensed key parts of his narrative into exhibit labels. During the afternoon the class worked with the exhibits department to produce the labels and mount the objects in a display case. The opening was that evening, at a reception for the Governor's Council on the Arts. It was an amazing experience, but you know, when we asked Roger for a title for this exhibit, he thought for a moment and simply said *Saquat*—"Objects." It was clear that these pieces themselves were only starting points for stories and didn't matter that much individually—that was the way he approached it.

SCHNEIDER: I think it is neat the way objects, in this case the parka, create an opening, an opportunity for retelling and how that retelling goes beyond a recounting of events to larger questions of identity, to a cultural interpretation and message about the past and the present. The message directs us to a proper relationship and treatment of the animals and the place where we live. This message, it seems to me, is what gives this story continued life; it is the "ultimate meaning" question that Jim raised early in our discussion. It explains, in part, why the story is retold. More than an event, more than an object, we are left with a lesson about life.

4

Singing and Retelling the Past

Kirin Narayan

Kirin Narayan is professor of anthropology at the University of Wisconsin in Madison. She grew up in India and moved to the United States at sixteen. Her major research has been in India, where she has been interested in women's songs since 1980. In this essay, she describes how she reintroduced a traditional women's wedding song to a group of friends and how they responded to the recording that had been made years before. While some of the verses to the song were not familiar to them, others were, and this leads to a discussion of underlying meanings in the song. The women share in a common tradition and also in the cultural expectation that they will sing songs at celebrations. The song, the setting, and the kin who are gathered offer a chance to share versions and participate in the reconstruction of old verses and a common tradition.

"These old memories are very lovable, they exist in such good songs," remarked Bimla Pandit, an accomplished singer, to her circle of female in-laws as I sat with them on a verandah, sipping tea and checking through song transcriptions. This association between narrative songs in the local dialect and past ways of life confronted me often in my work on women's songs in the Himalayan foothills of Kangra, Northwest India. In this essay, I use ethnographic materials from Kangra to explore a few ways that sung and spoken retellings of a folklore form can invoke the past: through linguistic terms; through the cultural logic of social practices; through chains of transmissions across generations and the conscious use of songs as teaching tools; and through marking an anthropologist's engagements across time. I focus my discussion around a women's song about Krishna's encounter with the gorgeous cowherd woman, Chandravali.

Krishna Stories in Kangra Women's Songs

Krishna is the eighth avatar or incarnation of the Hindu God Vishnu, Preserver of the Universe, who periodically takes form to rout evil. Krishna plays a central role in the epic *Mahabharata* (believed to have been composed somewhere between 300 B.C. and 300 A.D.) and in various Puranas. Episodes from Krishna's life are reread and retold in many languages, dialects, and genres across India. Among the most cherished stories are the miraculous events surrounding his birth; his childhood in a village, where he kills demons, gets into all kinds of mischief, and plays with other cowherd boys; his romantic relations with the *gopis*, the beautiful cowherd women; his elopement with Princess Rukmani just before her marriage to someone else; his overthrow of his wicked uncle King Kamsa; and the help he extends to the five Pandava brothers and their wife Draupadi, even serving as war charioteer for the second brother, Arjuna, and instructing him through the verses we know as the *Bhagavad Gita*.

Spreading out at the base of the towering Dhauladhar mountain range of the Western Himalayas, Kangra has long been linked with two deities associated throughout India with the mountains—the ascetic Shiva, who meditates in Himalayan snows, and Shiva's consort, Gaurja (or Parvati), daughter of the mountains, who is also the great Goddess. The spread of intense Krishna devotion through Kangra is more recent and appears to be linked to the reign of King Sansar Chand (1775–1823) when Kangra was a hill state. Sansar Chand was also instrumental in popularizing Krishna devotion through building temples to Krishna, painting murals, popularizing festivals like Janmashtami (Krishna's birthday), commissioning exquisite miniature paintings featuring the life and loves of Krishna, and patronizing performances relating to stories from Krishna's life (Archer 1973:286). William Moorcroft, a British traveler who visited Sansar Chand's court in 1820, noted that the king "in the evening hears music and frequently has Nachs [dance performances] in which the performers generally sing Brij Bhakha songs generally reciting the adventures of Krishna and those of the Gopees" (Archer 1973:262, expanding on Moorcroft 1971 (1841):144). Brij—or Braj—is the region in northern India associated with Krishna's childhood adventures and romantic liaisons with the *gopis*. "Brij Bhakha" refers to songs composed in the Braj regional dialect (*bhāshā*).

The spread of Krishna stories also appears to have inspired compositions in the Kangra dialect, called Pahari or Kangri. Certainly by the time of the scholar M. S. Randhawa's pioneering collection of Kangra folksongs made between 1951 and 1961, Krishna's presence was already established in multiple song genres. As Randhawa notes, "In these songs, Shri Krishna has a preeminent place" (1970:158). A full-scale analytic work in Hindi exploring the many dimensions of Krishna's identity in Kangra folksongs was subsequently undertaken by Meenakshi Sharma (1989), a local scholar and daughter of the prolific Kangra folklorist Dr. Gautam Sharma "Vyathit."

I have visited Kangra since I was a teenager, shortly before my American mother moved to a village there. I began writing down Kangra women's songs in 1980, during a year between college and beginning graduate school in cultural anthropology. I too almost immediately encountered songs featuring Krishna, first in the genre of bride's songs (*suhāg*) and then in subsequent years through other genres that include birth songs (*hansṇu khelṇu*), groom's songs (*sahere*), songs of suffering in married life (*pakharu*), and devotional song (*bhajan*). I learned that in Kangra, the word *gopi* is used interchangeably with the term "Gujari": that is, a woman of the Gujar Muslim pastoralist group associated with cows, buffalos, and the sale of milk products. The 1883–84 official British overview, *Gazetteer of the Kangra District,* draws on regional stereotypes to make a colonial typification of Gujaris; they are described as "tall and graceful in figure" and that moving about in public to sell milk products "unaccompanied by their husbands, undoubtedly exposes them to great temptations" (Punjab Government 1883–84:95). Following the partition of 1947 and creation of the new state of Pakistan, however, the Gujar presence in Kangra was diminished by emigration or brutal anti-Muslim violence. During my own years of association with Kangra, Gujaris were largely an imagined presence in Krishna songs indexing the past rather than in the lived landscape of everyday village interactions in the present.

Radha is perhaps Krishna's best-known *gopi*, or Gujari, and indeed many of the Kangra women's songs mention her by name. These portray her not just as his lover but sometimes also as his wife—a role usually associated with Rukmani. But Krishna's relationships with many other women are sung about too. My friend Urmila Devi Sood explained Krishna's prodigious romantic energy as the result of desires expressed by women who swooned over him in his previous incarnation as handsome Prince Ram, or Ramachandra.

> Krishna was always falling in love with women. Before he was born as Krishna, he had taken birth as Ramchandra. At the gathering of princes when Sita chose her groom, it was Ramchandra whom she got. All her girlfriends were absolutely incredulous. "Where did you get this groom from: Look at him! He's incomparable in looks, incomparable in wisdom, incomparable in every single thing. Where did you get this groom for yourself?" They were aflutter, ensnared by desire for him.
>
> So Ramchandra gave them a boon. He said, "In my next life, I'll marry you all."
>
> Radha is one of them, and there are many others that he married too … 108, it's said. (Narayan 1997:86)

While Urmilaji mentioned 108 *gopis*, other women estimated 360, or even 16,000. Among these was Chandravali, a name that can be glossed from Sanskrit as "collection of moons" or "moonlight." She is perceived as a woman so lovely that when she enters a town "there's a doubt whether the moon has risen or Chandravali Gujari has arrived. Her way of speaking, her gait, her style of draping her shawl and everything else about her is wonderfully attractive" (Sharma 1989:121). In order to get to know her, Krishna resorts to special wiles: disguising himself as a woman.

Chandravali's Song

I met Chandravali for the first time on a sunny morning in February of 1991, as I sat out in the courtyard of a Brahman settlement. I had been intermittently filling tapes with songs through almost four days of wedding festivities. For this wedding of a son, relatives had assembled from near and far, joining friends and neighbors. Women had been singing almost constantly—clustered close around ritual action, sitting on mats in rooms apart from the men, or dancing and prancing naughtily when the men departed with the groom's party. Women's presence in song was important to the event because in Kangra, as in much of India, women's songs are considered to bring good fortune to an occasion (cf. Henry 1988:110–11). Some steps of the rituals demanded certain descriptive songs that tended to repeat with different kinship terms inserted each round. Between these charged ritual moments, any generally appropriate song (for example, with a romantic theme) could be sung.

Most women's traditional songs in the Pahari dialect use a repetitive melody, with each line sung twice. This means that any woman—or group of women—might lead the song and that even someone who has never heard it before can join in for the repetition of each line. There is no fixed boundary, then, between performers and audience. Some women are said to have a *sukinni* or special predilection and interest in songs and are most likely to volunteer to lead. Others, though, might abstractedly mouth the words without much attention; else having fulfilled the ritual obligation of being present, they might turn to chatting in a low undertone.

"Women are always singing," observed one woman with a prodigious knowledge of songs. "You hear so many songs, but only some go sit inside your heart." Even among singers, then, repertoires of songs and versions of the same songs varied with individual predilection and also the kinds of songs that a singer was exposed to as a member of an extended family and resident in a village. Therefore, for women gathering together for ritual celebrations from different families and villages, it was a challenge to synchronize versions. Sometimes this involved a quick huddle of lead singers to work out a melody and a narrative line in advance; at other times, midway through the song singers would confront a divergence, and the version most loudly sung (or backed by more voices) would win out.

As is common at weddings, the groom was repeatedly compared to other celebrated bridegrooms of Hindu mythology: Ram, Krishna, and Shiva. Yet the songs emphasized not just the experience of the groom but also women related to him. As Susan Gal has observed, women's "voice" refers not just to the spoken word but also to perspectives on social relations that often diverge from representations stemming from dominant (male) groups (Gal 1991:176). Rich ethnographic work in other regions of India has shown how women's oral traditions challenge dominant ideologies of gender and of kinship (Flueckiger 1996; Raheja and Gold, 1994). This emphasis on female characters means that in women's folklore, mythological events are often recast to emphasize women's perspectives (Rao 1991).

By the fourth morning of wedding rituals, the groom's party had returned with the bride, and a big lunch feast was to be held in celebration. In the meanwhile, many of the guests were resting outdoors, seeking warmth in the sun. I sat out on a cotton rug with a group of women who had traveled from the groom's mother's village of birth. By now, my microphone had become part of the celebrations and had even been commandeered as a mock phallus for some bawdy skits that the women put on while the groom's party was gone. For days, various women older than me had been taking charge of my research, instructing me what to tape and what to ignore as "too filmi" (as in Bollywood film music). They had also been generously offering to "fill up" my tapes with their most cherished Pahari songs.

That morning, Sarla Upadhyay, a fine-featured woman in her fifties, took charge of my microphone and sang "Naglila" or "the snake play," a song that recounted how, as a boy, Krishna had vanquished the Serpent King Kaliya yet spared his life on account of the Serpent Queen Champa's petition. Sarla told me that many upper-caste women knew this song and might sing it as part of their morning routines. When I asked what genre of song this was, Sarla explained that this was a Gujari song, also known as *byāgaṛe* or a morning song. As other women had already explained to me, *gopis* in their Gujari form are associated with the mornings because that was when they used to go out to sell their milk, curds, or butter. Because cowherd women are celebrated for their devotion to Krishna, songs associated with them could also fit the larger genre of devotional *bhajan*.

Perhaps Sarla's mention of Gujaris was what prompted the groom's mother's half-sister, Suman, to take the microphone next. Suman was an animated woman in her late thirties, with a ready smile and dangling gold earrings. At a time when I was in my early thirties and regularly chastised for being unmarried, I had liked Suman at once, on our first meeting, when she declared that she was not married and was not interested in ever getting married, either. Grinning now, Suman started in on another song that she also identified as being of the genre of Gujari and morning song. She sang in a soft, clear voice, the melody weaving hypnotically. Her companions didn't seem to really know the song, though, and she didn't bother to repeat the lines twice. Instead, the others sat listening appreciatively. Each verse ended with the filler word *jī* —a form of respect that added to a rhyming, repetitive force. Occasional verses used a larger filler chunk, *bhalā jī* , which roughly translates as "how fine!"

The song begins with Krishna asking his wife, Rukmani, to loan him her physical form (*rūp*), but Rukmani says that forms can't be lent and offers him her ornaments instead.

dīye dīye rukmaṇ rupe de apaṇe bhes denā badalāi bhalā jī .
"Give, Rukmani,
give me your form.
I want to switch my looks."
How fine.

"Take my jewels, Krishna,
Take my silver ornaments too.
But you can't borrow a form."
How fine.

Krishna put on her jewels.
He put on her silver ornaments, too.
He switched his looks.
How fine.

All dressed up as a woman, Krishna makes his way to the Gujari Chandravali's village and looks around for her house.

Asking, seeking
He made his way through the lanes:
"Which is Chandravali's house?"

"Jasmine flowers in the courtyard,
A grand entrance, a verandah:
That is Chandravali's house."

Asking, seeking,
He arrived at the outer entrance:
"Is this Chandravali's house?"

"Jasmine flowers in the courtyard,
A grand entrance, a verandah:
This is Chandravali's house."

The promise of fragrance and beauty in the enclosed inner courtyard lures Krishna in through the outer entrance. When he arrives, he presents himself to Chandravali as her long-lost sister, but she is mystified.

"Come sister,
give me a hug:
Your little sister is here."
How fine.

"When were you born?
When were you married?
Since when have I had a little sister?"
How fine.

"When *you* were married,
Then *I* was born.
Since then you've had a little sister."
How fine.

Though puzzled, Chandravali is eager to be hospitable to this new-found sister, offering the traveler a hot bath and food.

"I'll fetch some cold water
and make it hot.
Come sister, let's take a bath."

"I've already bathed
in the Ganga and Yamuna.
Why don't you bathe and I'll scrub your back?"

"I'll winnow special *jhinjhan* rice
and cook us a meal.
Come sister, let's eat."

"I don't eat rice
on *ekādashi* days.
Why don't you eat and I'll feed you?"

Krishna is mimicking a pious woman who bathes in sacred rivers and fasts on appropriate days of the lunar cycle (like *ekādashi*, the eleventh day). He tenderly shows his sisterly affection by offering to scrub Chandravali's back and feed her with his own hands. Trusting in this loving sister, Chandravali makes up a bed for them, which is just what Krishna has come for. At first, he improvises an excuse for his male body, but as she touches different body parts in a speedy succession, he has no chance to account for himself.

> "I'll shake out the covers
> and prepare the bed.
> Come sister, let's sleep."

> First, Chandravali felt
> his legs:
> "Your legs are made like a man's!"

> "When I was young,
> mother died.
> Out grazing cattle, my feet became like a man's."

> Second Chandravali felt
> his head:
> "You have a man's lock!"

> Third, Chandravali felt
> his chest:
> "Your chest has a man's yellow shawl!

> Fourth, Chandravali felt
> his thighs:
> "You're wearing a man's cloth!"

All of the sudden, after his thighs are identified, the song's action changes to eating.

> "Eight measures of flour,
> Nine measures of ghee:
> Let's enjoy sweet pancakes and savory *pakoṛās* together."

In much Indian folklore, as A. K. Ramanujan has pointed out, eating is a sexual metaphor; as he writes, "The word for eating and (sexual) enjoyment have often the same root, *bhuj* in Sanskrit. Sexual intercourse is often spoken about as the mutual feeding of male and female" (Ramanujan 1982:272). Research among Krishna devotees in Govardhan, a major pilgrimage center associated with Krishna in North India, extends such an understanding of food to a devotional framework—as Paul Toomey (1990) observes, food is used as both a metaphor and a metonym for the intense emotions of love and devotion bonding Krishna and disciples.

Mixing up ghee and flour to fry delicious sweets and savories seemed evidence of Chandravali's assent to sharing sensual treats with Krishna. As Suman explained years later, with a significant look at Durga Pandit, her older half-sister, "He knows the night is going to be really long; he orders all this food so they can keep eating." "Oh, *that's it!*" responded her sister, shouting with laughter.

As Krishna and Chandravali share this prodigious amount of food, Chandravali's courtyard is visited by other women too. In what appears to be Krishna's voice, Chandravali is informed of her visitors:

> "A washerwoman has come to your courtyard.
> A half-year's heaps of clothes are to be washed:
> Wash them all in one night."

Asking for a half-year's worth of work to be performed, Krishna uses his powers to prolong the night to six months. The erotic connotations of this women's work were unexplained in the song, but rooted in cultural practice (cf. Toelken 1995:48–68). In 1991, washing clothes by hand while squatting by a stream still punctuated most village women's lives, and the short wooden bat they used while washing often stood in as a mock phallus in bawdy skits. No sooner than the washerwoman finishes her work of submerging, sudsing, thumping, rinsing, twisting, squeezing, and spreading out the huge pile of clothes, than another woman arrives:

> "A wool-carding woman comes to your courtyard.
> A half-year's worth of wool is to be carded:
> fluff it all in one night."

Again, the metaphor of carding was left to the imaginations of listeners who might have observed two brushes rubbing against each other, flattening, stroking, extending, and fluffing out wool until it was soft and light.

A whole year later, Chandravali remonstrates:

> "You tricked me once, Blue-black one,
> You tricked me twice.
> Turn this night into morning."
> How fine.

The song ended here, grins still sticking to the faces of the assembled women. Sarla observed that she had never heard this song in full before, and Suman explained, "I learned this from my mother."

With a literal earnestness I now wince to recall, I censoriously asked why, if Krishna tricked women this way, he should be worshipped. "Oh, it's not just Chandravali, he has 16,000 other *gopis*," the women sitting around Suman assured me. "Sixteen thousand or 360?" someone else asked. Gayatri Upadhyay, one of the other cousins-in-law present, quickly summarized a story in which the sage Durvas Rishi challenged Krishna, "If you're really pure and celibate then walk through the Yamuna river." Krishna walked right through, but when Durvas Rishi followed the waters closed up. "It's all God's *līla*, a divine play," the women agreed. In judging Krishna as a philandering man I had clearly missed the point: his charm and shape-shifting were all part of an ongoing cosmic playfulness between God and devotees (cf. Sax 1995). Indeed, the *gopis'* relations with him, where they often pine, can be viewed as an allegory of the soul's separation from God (Hardy 1983).

That morning though, Chandravali's song evoked the rich theme of sexual impropriety. As I often found, in the impromptu sequences of songs that emerged at gatherings, the intertextuality between songs could elaborate retellings around a particular theme. Krishna's encounter with Chandravali inspired the women to move on to another song that I taped in many variants, where a passing soldier is propositioned by a woman he addresses as Nainavali or "the one with the eyes." They then went on to sing about a woman whose libidinous younger brother-in-law tries to lure her into a tent, while her husband remains oblivious. Continuing with my ethnographic earnestness, I asked if such relationships ever happened between wives and their husband's younger brothers (it is a common theme in North Indian folklore). "Oh no!" the women assured me, "these things don't happen here." Gayatri reflected a moment, then suggested, "Maybe this happened to someone, sometime. And then we all sing about it."

I came to tape many versions of the songs about the bantering soldier and also of the horny brother-in-law, but the song of Chandravali remained a rare text for which I recorded no variant. Looking through libraries in the intervening years, I found mention of Chandravali—also spelled Candravali—as Radha's rival in Bengali compositions surrounding Krishna, indicating that she exists in other regional traditions beyond Kangra (Delmonico 1995; Wulff 1977). In a Bengali song, Krishna has failed to show up at a tryst with Radha; he has spent the night instead with Candravali, and shows up wearing her blue-silk sari (Wulff 1997:72–73). This song also echoes the theme of cross-dressing, though here it is the outcome rather than pretext for Krishna's liaison.

Chandravali With Oral Literary Criticism

Years went by without my encountering Chandravali again in the field. Her song clearly had wider circulation in Kangra, for Meenakshi Sharma's study of Krishna songs devotes two pages to Chandravali Gujari (1989:120–21). Although Sharma does not reproduce the text, her comments about Chandavali's identity indicate her knowledge of the same—or a similar—song. As Sharma writes, "In the whole group of Gujaris, Chandravali Gujari is so especially entrancing in her beauty that he [Krishna] takes on various forms to try and trick her. He is so keen to woo her that he even takes on the form of a woman. Although he's discovered in the end, he has accomplished his goal" (1989:120).

I continued to visit my mother and friends, and my continued interest in this song—and others—also resulted in retellings generated by my presence. Visiting Kangra in 2004, I took along a file of selected songs, including Chandravali's song, that I hoped to bring together in a book. My old friend and collaborator Urmila Devi Sood, or Urmilaji, was as always eager to look through and listen to songs. Leafing through my transcriptions in the Devanagari script, Urmilaji hit upon Chandravali's song.

"For so long I've been wanting to remember this song!" Urmilaji exclaimed, a smile breaking out over her face. She pulled the file closer, as though to embrace the text. "I didn't have anyone to sing it with, and I'd forgotten the root verse," she explained. "See, if you hear a song a lot, you make it your own, little by little. You remember the story, you sing the tune. But if you don't hear others sing it, you can forget how it goes."

Urmilaji's comment underlined that this song was rarely sung. Also, her words were a reminder that songs are a form of collective memory (Halbwachs 1980), sustained through cohorts of singers; indeed I often heard older women claim that if they had no one to reconstruct particular song texts with, they forgot the song.

Squinting at my transcription, Urmilaji recreated a singing community for herself. She sang to Suman's words though using a different melody. Coming across unfamiliar verses, she sometimes shook her head, inserting her own version. Having been reminded of how another woman sang, she was ready to share with me the song as she recalled it, complete with divergences from the text in her lap. She also elaborated on the song, treating me to her own oral literary criticism (Dundes 1966). As I had previously observed, for Urmilaji as for many other Kangra women, to explain a song was not to elaborate on symbolic depth but rather to retell it as a story, spelling out implicit meanings and logical connections (Narayan 1995).

Though Urmilaji was seeking to remember the root verse or *dhak* "from which the song grows its leaves and flowers," when she sang her own version, this starting verse turned out to be different, using the name Shyam—the dark-hued one—for Krishna.

> *dāḍi maniā shyām moochhā manāeā bhes liyā chandrāvalīā jī*
> Shyam shaved off his beard,
> he shaved his moustache.
> He took on the look of Chandravali.

Here Krishna's stripping of visible male marks is highlighted. Instead of borrowing his wife Rukmani's clothes and ornaments, he mirrors Chandravali's own beauty as her would-be sister.

Similarly, visiting Kangra in 2007, I stopped in to see Sangeeta Devi, a woman from Durga Pandit's settlement who had generously helped me during fieldwork almost fifteen years earlier. She had not been in good health in the intervening years and was practically blind, but she carried an air of amusement. As we chatted, we somehow got to talking about Chandravali, and Sangeeta Devi broke out into a laugh. She immediately began singing, as though being reminded of this song made its presence so compelling that it had to be unfolded to the very end. Her melody was closer to Suman's.

Sangeeta Devi's version told the familiar story but again a little differently. She elaborated on Krishna's transformation into a woman across five delightful verses: he orders eye makeup (*sūrmā*) and perfume (*attar*) from wandering peddlers; he orders a full, long skirt stitched with a brocade border; and he decorates a long wrap with gold spangles. Then, he paints a woman's *bindī* on his forehead and adorns himself in the sixteen ways of a married woman (*solah sringār*)—which would include earrings, bracelets, necklaces, ribbons, and various kinds of makeup. Then he sets out to cross the river. The boatman recognizes him despite his disguise, bemusedly asking why he, Krishna, should need a way across (playing on the image of salvation as "crossing over") and so Krishna jumps across the flowing Yamuna. The cowherds out grazing cattle and an old woman collecting dung cakes for fuel don't recognize him, though, when they tell him how to identify Chandravali's house. As usual, she's puzzled by a little sister showing up, and the song proceeds much as I had previously encountered it until they get into bed. After Sangeeta Devi observed, "We don't like to sing from here on when there are girls around," she launched into a fuller account of the dialogue between Chandravali and Krishna as she discerns that he is a man. He tells her that his feet became masculine after the austerities (*tapasyā*) that he did out in the forest (echoing a body of songs mentioning Goddess Gaurja's forest austerities to win her groom, Shiva). He tells her that he's wearing a man's cord around his waist because in the region he's from, it's now the custom for women to wear these too. He goes on to explain that his chest hasn't filled out because he hasn't yet bourne children. Though Sangeeta Devi omitted the sequence of cooking and eating together, and the visits from workers of different castes, she included verses I hadn't heard before. Chandravali's husband sits hunched over by the gateway as six months pass by without fresh food or water, and the cowherds hunch over, waiting out six months in the forest too.

Sangeeta Devi took great pleasure in the song, but she did not elaborate much beyond explaining unfamiliar words rooted in past practices: the wandering perfume sellers (*gāndhis*) who Krishna summons, the brocade border (*chhapuā lon*) on Krishna's skirt, and the man's waistcord (*tarāgi*) hidden under his disguise. She ended by commenting with a smile, "This was Krishna's *līla*, his play; he had so many queens, all his life."

Urmilaji, though, often expanded on songs through narrative commentary. She explained, "Chandravali was very beautiful and she did a lot of 'acting,' putting on airs." Using the English word 'acting,' Urmilaji seemed to portray Chandravali as a glamorous, slightly petulant film star. "She was haughty," Urmilaji continued. "She wouldn't talk to Krishna and so he decided to trick her." Urmilaji went on to describe how Krishna found Chandravali by the fragrant sandalwood tree (as opposed to Suman's jasmine bush) in her courtyard. The sweet scents—whether of sandalwood or jasmine—seem to surround Chandravali's lustrous allure. In Urmilaji's version, Chandravali sat spinning in the courtyard as

Krishna appeared. "In those days," Urmilaji commented, "women did a lot of spinning."

Assuring me that it was absolutely plausible that Chandravali might not have known that she had a younger sister, Urmilaji explained: "In the past, women would have nine or ten or twelve children. Daughters would grow up, and then the mother and the daughter would be giving birth at the same time. So one sister could have been born after another sister was married and if that sister were married far away, how would they know of each other? See, in the past, women were sometimes married so far away across the mountains that they might never be able to visit home in their whole lifetime. I've heard it said that when a bride came from far away, the wood for her cremation was packed in a bundle and sent at the time of her marriage!"

Urmilaji continued by noting that the fine *jhinjhan* rice that Chandravali cooks for Krishna was now displaced by other modern varieties and remembered only in songs. Coming to the washer-woman's arrival, Urmilaji observed that lower castes did not enter the house in the past but rather stood outside in the courtyard. She recounted how big bundles of clothes used to be kept for washermen engaged in service (*gaḍi kalothi/jajmāni*) relations with higher castes (cf. Parry 1979:67–70). In her version it was not just six months of clothes, but *twelve years* worth of clothes being vigorously washed through the night.

"Chandravali admits that Shyam has conquered her," Urmilaji concluded. "She says 'You tricked me this way, and you tricked me that way.' He tricked her first by arriving in the form of her sister. Then he tricked her again by making the night so long; twelve entire years long!"

While my transcriptions in the Devanagari script were a matter of delighted recognition, curiosity, and even amused comment by women singers like Urmilaji who could read, whenever I happened to bring out cassettes from previous years, these were greeted with an outpouring of emotion. Hearing the voices of old women who had since died could especially bring tears to the eyes of their surviving family members. Durga Pandit, a half-sister of Suman's (though not the groom's mother) even gathered relatives to listen to a tape of songs from an aunt-in-law who had passed on. Eyes downcast, somberly listening, the group of women then responded by singing related songs sparked by the same themes.

Visiting in 2004, I mentioned to Durga Pandit that I had taped her half-sister's song of Chandravali, and she wanted to hear it too. She knew of the song, she said, but she didn't know how to sing it; as she explained, her sister had been born of a different mother and they did not grow up singing the same songs together. I brought over the tape, and Durga Pandit borrowed her older daughter-in-law's portable tape recorder. She set this out on the verandah and started playing the tape, twiddling the knob to the highest volume. Her second daughter-in-law called us in to eat lunch just as the song began. I noticed nervously that this daughter-in-law's husband was home that day, already sitting cross-legged by the hearth with a rimmed steel *thālī* before him. Usually, women's songs were sung amid other women at ritual gatherings. I worried: would this graying, mild-mannered man find the song risqué? What were the ethics of my playing Suman's voice before a male in-law without asking her permission? "Shouldn't I turn the tape off?" I asked weakly, standing in the doorway. "Oh no, we'll listen as we eat," assured Durga Pandit. As her daughter-in-law ladled fragrant, steaming rice and aromatic dhal onto our steel *thālīs*, Durga Pandit cocked her head, smiling and laughing at Krishna's deceptions. Her son seemed oblivious, but I could not relax as I worried about inappropriate retellings in an altered context.

When I next visited, I found Durga Pandit all dressed up in a shiny gray synthetic outfit, all set to go out. "Is your taxi still here?" Durga Pandit enquired. "Let's go visit Suman!" It turned out that she also wanted to look in on a sick niece with appendicitis who lived in her sister's extended family home. We piled into the boxy van and wove our way for over an hour along the mountain roads, eventually emerging with gifts of fruit and biscuits, as well as my file of transcriptions and the tape containing Chandravali's song.

Suman greeted us with laughing warmth. After plying us with hot tea and refreshments, she asked what progress I had made through the years with my book on songs. We played the tape and she looked over my written version of her performance years earlier. There was one word I particularly hoped she could illuminate. When Krishna asks for his wife's jewels (*gahan*e) he also asks for her *bande*. Various women I had consulted when transcribing came up with different explanations for this archaic word—maybe this was really *boonde*, or teardrop earrings, they suggested. Else, elaborating on the word *band* or "fastened," they improvised that this could be some kind of belt or a blouse with ties at the back that women wore in the past. Suman thought it was a kind of silver ornament that women once wore, and so I abide by her gloss. The key issue was that Krishna borrowed women's clothes for his disguise.

Like Urmilaji and Sangeeta Devi, Suman explicated her song in terms of past practices. Remarking on the verse of Chandravali preparing the bed, she explained that in the past, mattresses were rolled up during the day and spread out for sleep. She also recalled the previous social hierarchy when lower castes came to the house to perform their services, explaining that this was why the washer-woman and the wool carder woman showed up in the courtyard.

"Mother used to sing this," she informed her teenage niece who was recuperating from her appendicitis operation and sat wanly looking on. "Mother said that her mother sang this song. It's an old song, from the old times."

"Do you and your sisters know this song?" I asked the niece.

She shook her head. "We don't know any of these old songs."

"These days girls are too busy studying and watching television!" asserted Durga Pandit, echoing a complaint I often heard older singers make. "The times have changed." I could only reflect how different everyone's lives—including mine—had been in the early 1980s, when I first became interested in collecting Kangra songs, and television was unknown in the valley. At that time, local songs had been part of a taken-for-granted aspect of ritual life; although songs contained the past then too, there seemed to be a greater continuity with that past. By the twenty-first century, though, the imaginative break engineered by education in the national lan- guage and widespread exposure to other sorts of lives through the media had rendered local songs such as Chandravali's as clearly belonging to a past time.

Retelling the Past

That oral history can be transmitted through folklore genres is an established insight (Scheub 1987; Tonkin 1992; Vansina 1985). Here I have explored a song of a genre where mythological pres- ence spills into legendary time, evoking a generalized past rather than any particular historical events. Although none of the singers I knew claimed Chandravali as a real historical figure living in a particular Kangra village, nonetheless, *byāgaṛe* or Gujari as a genre of Pahari song seemed saturated with a connection to a regional past. This connection has several dimensions.

First, the past can be summoned up in the very linguistic terms present in a text. In the case of Chandravali, I learned about the concrete details of bygone kinds of clothes and ornaments, varieties of rice, ways of making beds, and forms of labor associated with particular castes. The very term "Gujari" for the kind of song was a painful reminder of the current absence of Muslim Gujars in most Kangra villages and would sometimes evoke stories of which areas of villages they had lived in. With downcast eyes and hushed voices, older women would sometimes remember how Partition in 1947 led many Gujars to migrate across the mountains to the newly formed state of Pakistan while others who stayed on were brutally murdered amid anti-Muslim riots.

Second, the plot of the song drew on practices and feelings associated with the past, for example child marriage, the lack of communication across distances in the mountains, the hospitality lavished on visitors walking far distances, and caste relations that led lower castes to the courtyards of their patrons. To understand why people behaved in particular ways in the song, then, was to recall how ancestors had once lived. Retelling the story of Chandravali, singers spoke not of Krishna mythology set in the Braj region, but of the ways their ancestors had lived in Kangra.

Third, the transmission of a song linked a singer backward in time with female exemplars and co-performers. Women often spoke about how their songs connected them to other women of the past— beloved relatives and generalized women alike. Suman, for example, linked her performance to her mother and grandmother. Similarly, an old woman I called Tayi, or Aunty, told me that through singing, "you get some solace (*tasallī*) in your heart, that there have been times like this for other hearts in the past." Yet even as the songs carried a connection to the past, they also could be used as a commentary on the present, offering moral instruction to younger women. As one woman said, "Suppose I bring a daughter-in-law here tomorrow, she'll say [in a delicate, lowered voice] 'Hah! My mother-in-law is terrible! She does this, she does that.' But if I convey these songs to her then it'll come into her brain, 'Oh no! Oh brother! These people had even worse times than me. My situation is good after all! I shouldn't carry on this way.' Do you understand now? It's for this reason that stories of the past, the songs of the past, should be listened to, should be sung, transmitted from one person to another so the singers can say, 'Look at the hardships! These are such wonderful songs. Such touching songs!'"

Fourth, my own attempts to record this oral tradition amid the flow of time establishes it as oral history; as Schneider has pointed out, "[O]ral history is both the act of recording and the record that is produced" (2002:62). My own returns to Kangra through time and attempts to find illumination on this text were folded into the memories carried with retellings, and sparked further retellings. By eliciting versions, commentaries, and comparisons, scholars themselves clearly generate retellings from others in the field. At the same time, scholars produce their own retellings in translations across languages and into publications.

I have focused on how this song points backward, over the horizon of a vanished past, and moves forward through channels, like this volume, that may include an anthropologist's transmutations. Equally one could explore how a song evokes shared cultural assumptions that endure through time and space, for example the figure of the endlessly surprising and adorable divine prankster, Krishna. The first morning that I heard Suman sing, I had tried to draw her out into more commentary. I asked, "But *why*? Why does Krishna trick Chandravali?"

Suman had shrugged, laughing. "He's Krishna, after all!" she said, implicitly invoking a rich cultural history of retellings.

Acknowledgments

I am grateful to many sources of funding that have supported my field research and prior publications on Kangra: the American Institute for Indian Studies, National Endowment for the Humanities, School of American Research, John Simon Guggenheim Foundation, Social Science Research Council, University of Wisconsin Graduate School, H. I. Romnes Fellowship funds and Women's Studies Research Center, University of Wisconsin. I am grateful to William Schneider for the invitation to write this paper for the 2004 Oral History Association meetings in Portland, and to Patricia Partnow for serving as our discussant. I thank Margaret Beissinger, Kenneth George, Joanne Mulcahy, V. Narayana Rao, William Schneider, and Barre Toelken for inspiring and critical comments on earlier versions of this essay.

References

Archer, William G. 1973. *Indian Paintings from the Punjab Hills: A Survey and History of Pahari Miniature Paintings.* Vol I. Delhi: Oxford University Press.
Delmonico, Neal. 1995. How to Partake in the Love of Krishna. In *Religions of India in Practice.* Donald S. Lopez, Jr., ed., 246–68. Princeton, NJ: Princeton University Press.

Dundes, Alan. 1966. Metafolklore and Oral Literary Criticism, *The Monist* 60:505–16.

Flueckiger, Joyce. 1996. *Gender and Genre in the Folklore of Middle India.* Ithaca, NY: Cornell University Press.

Gal, Susan. 1991. Between Speech and Silence: The Problematics of Research on Language and Gender. In *Gender at the Crossroads of Knowledge.* M. di Leonardo, ed., 175–203. Berkeley: University of California Press.

Halbwachs, Maurice. 1980. *The Collective Memory.* New York: Harper and Row.

Hardy, Friedhelm. 1983. *Viraha-Bhakti: The Early History of Krsna Devotion in South India.* Delhi: Oxford University Press.

Henry, Edward. 1988. *Chant the Names of God: Music and Culture in Bhojpuri-Speaking India.* San Diego: San Diego State University Press.

Moorcroft, William, 1971 (1841). *Travels in the Himalayan Provinces of Hindustan and the Panjab.* H. H. Wilson, ed. New Delhi: Sagar Publications.

Narayan, Kirin. 1995. The Practice of Oral Literary Criticism: Women's Songs in Kangra, India. *Journal of American Folklore.* 108: 243–64.

Narayan, Kirin, in collaboration with Urmila Devi Sood. 1997. *Mondays on the Dark Night of the Moon: Himalayan Foothill Folktales.* New York: Oxford University Press.

Parry, Jonathan. 1979. *Caste and Kinship in Kangra.* London: Routledge.

Punjab Government. 1883–84. *Gazetteer of the Kangra District.* Calcutta: Calcutta Central Press Company.

Raheja, Gloria, and Ann Gold. 1994. *Listen to the Heron's Words: Reimagining Gender and Kinship in North India.* Berkeley: University of California Press.

Ramanujan, A. K. 1982. Hanchi: A Kannada Cinderella. In *Cinderella: A Folklore Casebook.* Alan Dundes, ed., 259–75. New York and London: Garland.

Randhawa, M. S. 1970. *Kangra: Kala, Desh aur Geet. [Kangra: Art, Region, and Song].* New Delhi: Sahitya Academy.

Rao, V. Narayana. 1991. A Rāmāyaṇa of Their Own: Women's Oral Tradition in Telugu. In *Many Ramayanas: Diversity of a Narrative Tradition in South Asia.* Paula Richman, ed., 114–36. Berkeley: University of California Press.

Sax, William, ed. 1995. *The Gods at Play: Līla in South Asia.* New York: Oxford University Press.

Scheub, Harold. 1987. Oral Poetry and History. *New Literary History* 18:477–96.

Schneider, William. 2002. … *So They Understand: Cultural Issues in Oral History.* Logan, Utah: Utah State University Press.

Sharma, Meenakshi. 1989. *Lokgiton mein Krishna kā swarūp: kangrā janpad ke sardarbh mein [Krishna's Identity in Folksongs in the Context of the Kangra folk].* New Delhi: Taksheela Prakashan.

Toelken, Barre. 1995. *Morning Dew and Roses: Nuance, Metaphor, and Meaning in Folksongs.* Urbana and Chicago: University of Illinois Press.

Tonkin, Elizabeth. 1992. *Narrating Our Pasts: The Social Construction of Oral History.* Cambridge: Cambridge University Press.

Toomey, Paul. 1990. Krishna's Consuming Passions: Food as Metaphor and Metonym for Emotion at Mount Govardhan. In *Divine Passions: The Social Construction of Emotion in India.* Owen M. Lynch, ed., 157–81. Berkeley: University of California Press.

Vansina, Jan. 1985. *Oral Tradition as History.* London and Nairobi: James Currey and Heinemann.

Wulff, Donna. 1997. Radha's Audacity in Kirtan Performances and Women's Status in Greater Bengal. In *Women and Goddess Traditions in Antiquity and Today.* Karen L. King, ed., 64–83. Minneapolis: Fortress Press.

Singing and Retelling the Past

A Conversation with Kirin Narayan and
Barre Toelken

Kirin Narayan and Barre Toelken explore how songs
can go beyond meaning to carry a commonly shared
sense of experience; they can be part of our lived
experience, even in cases where we have not directly
experienced the event or activity described. Songs,
and this applies to stories as well, do more than enter-
tain or inform about an event; they create opportunities to be part of a shared performance, a form of
participation that engenders a sense of identification
with the tradition. In Narayan's Chandravali song,
the women from the region identify with and experience the song in familiar ways, even though they
do not share knowledge of all the same verses. The
experiences they do share create a social bond that
reinforces their "collective relationship." In a similar
way, Toelken uses the example of the ballad "Rolling
Home," which for him and his relatives evokes a common family bond that goes back to the whaling days.

SCHNEIDER: Let's begin by asking how songs are a special way of
invoking the past.

TOELKEN: Well, let me start with how songs help to carry on the
past. In my own family there were people who went to sea; they
were whalers in the 1860s and 70s. I don't think anyone in the family has been to sea in the generations since then, yet they all still
sing these whaling songs. And when they do, their eyes change. It
is as if they are reexperiencing something they never experienced.
Does that make any sense? The song has managed to carry down

Barre Toelken is professor of folklore at Utah State University Press. For
many of us, Toelken has been our primary introduction to folklore and
the role it plays in our own lives. Some of us have been fortunate enough
to hear him play folk music and talk about the role the songs play in oral
tradition. His academic contributions are well known. *The Dynamics of
Folklore* (1996) and *The Anguish of Snails* (2003) are examples of his work.

some experience for them that they actually didn't have, but they can have through the song. It's not the same bone wearying experience of being out at sea on a whaler, but it is an experience nonetheless, and I think that's something that ought to be examined more with all folksongs. Until recently, folksongs were thought of as just a way of seeing the past as opposed to experiencing the past. The experiences I am describing here are more a way of keeping the past alive in our lives or keeping the near end of the past in our own experience, in our mouth, so we have some way of continuing to experience it.

SCHNEIDER: Wow, that's super, Barre. I think the idea of experiencing—in the sense of being able to imagine and relate oneself to the song, as opposed to being a distant listener—may be similar to what happens when someone tells you a story one-on-one. In that kind of storytelling, the teller re-creates an experience. The storyteller's performance allows us to experience more than the words; we will remember the context of the sharing, the way the teller constructed the story, and our emerging relationship with the speaker. He or she becomes part of the story, our link to the events described. We feel and sense where the person is coming from and where they are trying to take us. In a sense they have invited us into the story.

TOELKEN: There's one song, "Rolling Home," that a lot of groups still sing, but our family sings it and I think there are two verses that I hadn't heard until recently because nobody in the family can sing them without crying. And yet no one in the family has ever experienced the events described in the verses. So, that's a mystery to me. I learned those verses when I was about sixty-five and I'm almost crying now when I'm talking about it. There's an emotional connection, a load that goes beyond what you described, Bill. The song reaches to some shared experience, a bond that we share as a family, a bond that was created years ago and while I can tell you about it, you can't experience it like I do.

I'll give you an example that parallels it in a way. Everyone in my family, including me, has a tattoo on their right shoulder and that is something that goes back to sailing times. I don't think anybody's been sailing since the 1900s. So this tradition of having your shoulder tattooed, and it has to be a particular tattoo, creates a commonly shared experience.

NARAYAN: What I see as the parallel between your description and mine is a sense of continuity with one's progenitors through imaginative participation in their experience, whether through the performance of a song or through the visible mark on one's shoulder. The sharing of voices blended in a song allows the participants of a group to maintain a collective relationship to the past. There is also something quite magical about singing, as voices join together and become larger than the parts.

TOELKEN: Yes, the songs we are discussing, and the people who sing them, do something special: they take you out of the present context that you share with too many people and put you back in a context that you share with a precise group of people. And now that people are moving much more, maybe the singing is one way they have to get back to a set of people that were formative in their lives.

NARAYAN: Barre, as I think about my Kangra material, your example of a family tradition reminds me of how some of the songs I have worked with in Kangra are also passed down within the family, but also many of the songs speak from a regional tradition, from shared cultural assumptions that transcend particular families. I think I mentioned how when people come from entirely different villages knowing different versions of the song, they have to work out who will be the dominant singer. Sometimes verses get left out and sometimes people take me aside afterwards and say, "*They* didn't sing it properly." Occasionally there is some tension between households. A mother-in-law and her daughters-in-law might not approve of a version sung by another family group. Sometimes a group will take a song off on a tangent, and when it rejoins the main current of words that others are familiar with, they will join in again. That's why collecting variants of songs across the valley was endlessly fascinating.

TOELKEN: It means that the variants are not just variants; they are parts of the same song sung for different reasons and coming from different places.

NARAYAN: That's so true about place. Women are usually married outside of the village where they were born—so singers are often carrying verses between villages.

SCHNEIDER: Yet despite the variations, the songs evolve over hundreds of years and maintain their identity and they continue to be resung.

TOELKEN: To understand why they persist we should look at the way the songs are sung. Kirin, your description of the repeated lines may point to a strong element that allows and encourages participation, even by those who don't recall the exact words of each verse. The singer sings one line and then others sing that line again. So there's no fixed boundary between the performers and the audience, and if you are an insider the boundary between your experience and that of the performer is minimized. I think it is significant that that is a feature of the folksong complex in Kangra society.

NARAYAN: Another key factor in the perpetuation of the tradition is the fact that the songs are required. Women *must* sing to make the occasion auspicious, for good fortune. The kinds of songs they choose to sing, though, are changing.

SCHNEIDER: It is appropriate to point out in conclusion that both of you have lived your life not just studying stories but living with them, living as part of insider groups where you are privy to know the cultural assumptions and to participate in the tradition in ways that deeply affect your life and identity. Retelling, or in this case res-inging, is a way to participate in your history: to use Barre's term, a way to "reexperience" one's history.

5

The Weight of Faith

Generative Metaphors in the Stories of Eva Castellanoz

Joanne B. Mulcahy

Joanne B. Mulcahy teaches at the Northwest
Writing Institute at Lewis and Clark College in
Portland, Oregon. Her degrees are in folklore,
anthropology, and comparative literature. In
this essay she describes how Eva Castellanoz, a
Mexican artist and *curandera* (traditional healer)
living in Oregon, uses metaphors to generate
stories that instruct and inspire diverse audiences. Mulcahy describes the settings where Eva
Castellanoz employs the properties of trees as a
way to talk about healing, faith, and models for
living. This central metaphor, which connects to
the Mexican Tree of Life symbol, has cultural and
personal resonance for Castellanoz and provides a
means for sharing her understandings with others.

As a child in Mexico, and later growing up in Pharr, Texas, Eva
Castellanoz loved poetry. As an adult, she mastered its central tool:
metaphor. Of faith, Eva says, "How do you measure it? Can you
say, 'Today I have ten pounds?'" Contrasted with faith's immea-
surability, Catholicism is rigid: a "dress that doesn't fit anymore."
The "root and bark" of her Mexican heritage, Eva says, are being
"stripped and bitten away" by life in America. These and other metaphors created from social life and the natural world are the hooks

on which Eva's stories hang. They emerge from her life as a teacher, *curandera*, folk artist, mother, and grandmother. Eva's stories range over a variety of topics, but the same interlocking metaphors recur. Discussions of faith intersect with the parallel "branch" metaphor of a tree, its roots and bark. These are part of a larger conceptual system Eva draws on to talk about the meaning of her life and work in a culturally specific way.[1]

Much of the research on retellings focuses on repetition of the same story in multiple contexts and the relationship between oral and written versions.[2] In this essay, I explore instead the constancy of metaphors that generate different stories about faith in four different contexts. In each setting, the metaphor prompts a story from Eva's repertoire, revealing her verbal artistry in responding to the needs of an audience.[3] The recurrence of the tree metaphor is significant. First, the tree of life is a central symbol in Mexican folk art, integrating indigenous traditions of the Maya, Mixtec, and Aztec with images from European Catholicism.[4] Trees are also a widespread metaphor of "vitality and self-regenerative power" and provide potent symbols of collective identity (Rival 1998:1–3). Eva's stories spurred by tree metaphors reproduce and reshape her family's history and heritage for subsequent generations.

Stories about faith cover varied topics: traditions passed down by Eva's parents; her family's life in Mexico, Texas, and Oregon; pride in her Mexican heritage, arts, and healing practices; and stories about Nyssa's young gang members. In each case, her individual stories point to broader social issues, while traditional tales encompass personal dimensions. Contexts vary from our tape-recorded conversations to talks for community groups. Settings discussed here include my initial interviews with Eva in her home (1992); further conversations in a hotel in Portland (1998); a community gathering at an arts center in Enterprise, a town in northeastern Oregon (2002); and a meeting at the trailer that houses her youth program in Nyssa (2004).

Stories about faith also place Eva in a cross-cultural world of storytellers who offer spiritual and practical instruction through narrative (Lawless 1993; Narayan 1989; McCarthy Brown 1991). Some of Eva's teachings educate outsiders about Mexican and Mexican American life; others suggest "key scenarios" for the Latino community, "clear-cut modes of action appropriate to correct and successful living" (Ortner 1973:1341).

Photo copyright Jan Boles

Eva holding a bouquet of her handmade wax and paper flowers. These might be used for an upcoming wedding or another
rite of passage. She uses the same wax and paper flowers
to make *coronas*, the floral crowns central to weddings, and
quinceañeras, young women's fifteenth-birthday celebrations.

Background: A Mexican Healer in Oregon

I've known Eva since 1989: as a co-worker in documenting Latino
folk arts in Oregon, as a friend, and as a collaborator in recording
her life story. When we met, I was director of the Oregon Folk Arts
Program, and she had just received a National Heritage Award for
her *coronas* (wax and paper floral crowns used for young women's
fifteenth-birthday *quinceañera*). When I discovered that Eva had
cancer and was not expected to live, I began recording her stories
in 1992. Fourteen years and many interviews later, Eva has not only
survived but has thrived as a nationally recognized folk artist and

teacher. She is widely acknowledged as well for *curanderismo*, a complex system that incorporates aspects of Spanish-Arabic traditions and indigenous Mexican medicine (Trotter and Chavira 1997). Television documentaries and National Public Radio programs have chronicled her life. She has received numerous awards, and for four years she was a member of the Oregon Arts Commission. Now, Eva frequently speaks at conferences and events concerning Latinos in Oregon and Idaho.

Our friendship has changed over sixteen years, yet it still brims with the contradictions and complexities, the shared understandings and differences, of cross-cultural relationships. We share status as women of Catholic heritage committed to Oregon, yet our differences are substantial. Eva recounts hardships I cannot imagine: poverty, illness, the loss of five siblings and a son, the murder of a granddaughter, and many years of migration and dislocation. In the mix of similarities and differences a hybrid world emerges, one important to feminist ethnographers willing to explore the emotional connections forged in fieldwork.[5] Raised within but disillusioned with the institutional church, I find solace in Eva's evocation of faith outside formal doctrine. From our first meeting, I wanted to understand Eva's belief in the world's possibilities. How had her faith, inscribed in both religious and secular terms, remained so constant in a life assaulted by hardship? How had her artful metaphors, crafted to express such belief, taken shape over a lifetime?

Eva was born in Valle de Santiago, Guanajuato, Mexico. When she was two years old, her family moved to Pharr, Texas, in the Rio Grande Valley after the death from disease of her five older siblings. Her father had already worked in different parts of Oregon for many years as part of the *bracero* program that brought Mexican workers north during World War II (Gamboa 1995). The family traveled back and forth from Texas to Oregon as migrant workers before finally settling in Nyssa, a predominantly Latino agricultural community on the Oregon-Idaho state line. In 1957 when Eva arrived, she was a young wife pregnant with the first of her nine children. There were few Latino families permanently settled in Oregon then. But as the Hispanic population has grown, Eva and her family have played increasingly important roles in the community. All her children started out picking sugar beets and onions. Most have now moved to employment in banks, government services, and the Amalgamated Sugar Company where the beets are processed. Her son Diego, a foreman in the factory, was also the first Latino mayor of Nyssa. Despite their growing strength in numbers and political power, Latinos in the valley still encounter racism, as Eva frequently recounts. Still, Eva asserts her family's sense of place in eastern Oregon as "the realization of my daddy's dream" and describes Nyssa as "my piece of the puzzle."

Can Faith Be Measured? Four Contexts

Nyssa, Oregon, July 2, 1992

> I have to live faith. I cannot weigh faith, I cannot measure it.

We're sitting on Eva's patio, cool even on this steamy July day when the temperature has soared past one hundred degrees. I have come east from Portland, as I have for the three years since we met. In between visits, we keep in touch by phone and mail. This time, with a grant from the Oregon Humanities Council, I will stay for a month to record her stories, hoping to learn enough to communicate to outside audiences. Eva and I are alone, so there isn't a literal audience. But Eva knows that I will write about our discussion. An implied audience hovers, a third party of potential readers shaping the storytelling context.

Eva brushes back her permed black hair, gray just touching the edges of her temples. Her smooth amber skin is barely lined. In white jeans and a Mexican embroidered top, she could easily pass for far younger than her fifty-three years. Beyond the house is the small *casita* surrounded by rows of zinnias, sunflowers, zucchinis, and tomatoes that stretch back to the edge of the nearby Snake River. Here, Eva heals people and makes her *coronas*. In the future, I will spend many more hours at Eva's house—in the kitchen eating homemade tortillas or sleeping in the Guadalupe Room crammed with religious icons and family photographs. But perhaps no setting will be as central as this patio next to a huge locust tree that Eva now points to, saying,

> This tree that does not talk taught me the biggest lesson of my life. It was sick and dying; it had no leaves. . . . An old Mexican man told my husband to drill a hole in its trunk and soak a stake with a special recipe and drive it through that hole. So he did. In about a month the tree started to heal [from the solution that had dripped down to the roots]. I learned that when the root is ruined, the limbs are sick, like our heritage that has been stripped and bitten away.

The cross and koi pond in Eva's yard rest near the *casita* where she makes *coronas* and helps those who come for healing.

This is the first time I hear Eva describe the tree with healthy roots as an extended metaphor for the importance of heritage. She frequently invokes the tree in speaking with local farm workers who learn to abandon their traditional practices in the U.S. Eva tells them the story of her family's move out of Mexico, when her father said that no one could ever "take Mexico out of them." Further, since Eva's heritage is Otomí and Nahua (Aztec), she feels particular affinity with the many migrant workers from indigenous groups.[6] She tells them:

> Be yourself. This is who you are. Never leave the root. Because once you do, you start to die to yourself. Otherwise, God would have made us all the same. He wanted me to be a Mexicana and to look how I look. . . . No matter what happens in my life, I know who I am and I'm happy at my root and that helps me.

Part of Eva's "roots" is an indigenous faith outside institutional religion. "Because we were wetbacks, we didn't go to church," Eva says of her childhood in Texas. "We didn't go anywhere. My parents had their little rituals at home. But they were very believing people, which I am very thankful for. They taught me because they believed, truly."

In these first interviews, Eva lays out the pivotal elements of her worldview around the framework of faith: knowing one's roots and attending to the rituals, history, and culture of one's people. Still, since I don't initially understand the depth or shape of Eva's stories, I look for tools. Feminist scholars have offered ways to read women's stories, revealing pattern in seemingly redundant refrains (McCarthy Brown 1991), uncovering the "unsaid" through "intratextual" interpretation of key metaphors (Lawless 1993), and linking stories and material culture as dual articulations of self and society (Babcock 1993). Briggs points out that when discourse lacks "textuality," certain signs become critical to interpretation (1988:91). In Eva's stories, these signs are her repeated metaphors that signal the listener to pay attention. Slowly, I begin to understand how Eva's tree metaphor communicates her message through its component symbols: the roots of the tree, though invisible, are the foundation; the trunk and its bark are symbols of potential transformation; the leaves are the most visible, renewable manifestation of culture. These components of the tree will emerge repeatedly in Eva's stories as she urges listeners toward understanding and potential change. For one of the possibilities of metaphor is the creation of new meaning, the "intersection of what has been and what can be" (Becker 1997:60). Eva's stories of faith pivot on metaphors that evoke the powerful aspects of tradition but also urge new cultural meaning.

Portland, Oregon, November 13, 1998

> Faith—who can measure it? Can we take a ruler and say, "I have two feet today. Or I have one pound or ten. Or it tastes of what—raspberries?" Can Catholicism do it? Or Methodist or Baptist? I think faith can only be lived.

In the Hilton Hotel on a blustery autumn day, Eva returns to the theme of faith, this time integrating family stories, her mother's folklore about healing, and a critique of Catholicism. We're meeting at an arts-in-education conference where teachers from throughout the Northwest have gathered to watch Eva make *coronas*, the wax and paper floral crowns for which she is now well known. Later in the hotel room, we discuss an essay I'm writing about her life for *Legacy of Hope*, a book on Catholics and social change in Oregon. When I ask for her thoughts about Catholicism, Eva contrasts the Church with her parents' faith.

> My parents were very, very Catholic. They were not only Catholic by name, but they are a people of very pure faith, believers in God.... They had so much faith by their deeds, not only their words.

"Not only their words" refers to Eva's ongoing critique of the institutional church and the failure of clergy and others to address poverty, illness, and the material needs of the faithful. In contrast, Eva turns to stories about her mother's faith, exemplified by healing with the mesquite bark, extending the "root of tradition" metaphor:

> She [Eva's mother] said, "God will give me the strength. God will give me the way." People would come to her for healing. Sometimes, she didn't have time to do this or gather that. She would say, "Go get me some bark from the mesquite." And I would. By that time, I knew that this was not right for the ailment of that person. But they would be healed. "Mama, you shouldn't have given her that mesquite bark because that was not her problem." "Mi'ja, I didn't have anything else. And by faith. . . ."
>
> Then she would tell me this story. One time there was this man who was a drunk and he wanted money to drink. So he went around telling people that if they gave him some money, he would go to Jerusalem where our Lord was crucified and bring them a little bark of the cross. So people would give him money. He would go off and drink it. One day, he came back and someone said, "Hey, it's been a long time and you never brought us our bark from Jerusalem." So he goes to this mesquite, you know, and gets all this bark and gives it to the people. And this man was supposed to be dying and the devil was about to take him. This is the story. And the man took out his little bark and showed it to the devil and the devil laughed and said, "Your faith is what kills me, not your bark."
>
> This woman [Eva's mother] raised people out of beds where doctors said, "No more." At least three that I truly saw and know of because of faith, the faith that she infused to people because she had it. And not only words, you know.

Eva embeds this traditional tale—"one time there was"—between two accounts about her mother. The tale is handed down from her parents to Eva as witness, and now to us, her audience. In both sets of stories, Eva explores the symbol of the bark as the malleable, available aspect of culture. It can be broken off, used, even deceptively traded. But the deeper, enduring "root" of faith cannot. The tree/bark metaphor generates stories that can be interpreted differently. Eva knows that at least some of the readers of this book on social change will be Oregon's Hispanic Catholics. Religious listeners will connect to biblical aspects of this tale, including the raising of the sick from their beds. Yet others may bring secular meaning to the story. My own interpretation bridges the two, poised between the shared symbols of Catholicism and my attempts to interpret Eva's stories as cultural narratives.

   The connection of faith to healing locates Eva's stories in a larger world of narrative. Metaphors of illness and healing animate accounts from numerous cultures. Where the "sickness" of local cultures has been used to justify political control, the metaphor of healing is a counterargument that has become perhaps "the most frequent and most effectively deployed weapon against colonial discourse" (Olmos and Paravisini-Gebert 2001:xx). Other studies reveal how healing is an often-invoked metaphor for resistance to colonialism (cf. Napoleon 1991; Mulcahy 2000). Such stories are healing in part because they harness a usable past in the service of the present, choosing to emphasize particular threads of complex histories.

   Further, Eva's stories reach for coherence in a life that has been consistently disrupted by moving, tragedy, and economic uncertainty. The use of metaphor helps form a coherent vision of a life and may inspire a changed perspective on "cultural phenomenon that impedes resolution of disruption" (Becker 1997:60). In Eva's case, this includes reforming her personal faith in the context of failures of the Catholic church to meet community need.

Enterprise, Oregon, October 18, 2002

   I'm going to share with you first what to me is healing. Healing starts with yourself. Does anybody know how much faith weighs? Have you weighed it, anyone? Can you say, "Yesterday, I had ten pounds. Today I only have one"? Can anybody measure it—I had this much, but now I have this much? Can anybody taste it, like we're tasting food today?
   We can only give it. My people and I live it day by day. We may plan; I may have a calendar and say—even through the year, I'm amazed to see people planning through the year—but Mexicanas, mañana. No time. I hardly ever carry a watch, just rely totally on trust. I walk, maybe the next step I will fall. But I trust I won't. To me, that's healing.

Eva holds an audience of about forty people in thrall at the Fishtrap House in Enterprise, a town in northeast Oregon's Wallowa Mountains. Gathered here are farmers and ranchers; artists who work for Fishtrap, a local literary organization with a national reach; and a growing group of artists drawn to this region of lustrous lakes and snowcapped mountains. I've come with Eva to hear her talk about Day of the Dead traditions and her healing practices. We arrived in town separately, Eva's ever-problematic car dying just as she got here. But she spontaneously weaves the car story as an occasion for faith into her narrative, followed by a traditional tale about "miracles":

My car's in a mess. She [Joanne] says, "Don't worry." Some people say "Eva is dumb" because I trust. To me, that's the first thing I ever learned. It has been very, very helpful in my life. Trust. Things happen for a reason.

Stories help me a lot. I grew up with stories, with my three siblings and our parents telling us stories about where we came from.

One story that I want to share this morning is that there was this very rich person that had all this land. One day, a person who was called the master walked into that land without knowing it. To that master, there were no boundaries. He had this child with him who was following the master to see what he did and what he could learn. They met the owner of the place who said, "What are you doing here? This is my land. . . . Well, I have heard a lot about the miracles that you have made."

"Oh, I didn't know that," the master said.

The owner said to the master, "Well, I have been walking for a while and I am very thirsty. Make water! Since you can make miracles, make water. I am the owner, you're on my land, and I'm thirsty."

The master says, "Did you see the sun rise this morning?"

"Yes, what does that have to do with me needing water?"

They kept on walking, almost the whole day. The landowner was hungry, he was thirsty, he was tired, and he wanted to see these miracles. And the master didn't make miracles. The man got tired and left.

The master continues to walk with the child and he finds a rabbit lying on the ground. He picks him up, blows on him, and the rabbit starts running. The child says, "Wow!" The master finds a bird that's sick. He catches the bird, kisses the bird, puts him out, and he flies. They were hungry and thirsty, so they sat down. He tapped on the trunk of a tree, and there's water. The child says, "Why didn't you do this when the man was asking you?" He says, "If you don't believe in the sunrise, you can't believe in miracles, so what's the use?"

That story taught me to believe in the sunrise, and you are looking at a miracle right now. I look into miracles in my own close and extended family. We know, and I say "we" meaning my people. I was speaking to herbs and seeing miracles since I was in my mother's womb. Both my parents were healers. I saw my father pray to the trees and to the plants and ask them permission to take just what he needed. I saw my mother run to the tree because she didn't have what that person needed that day. I would even tell her, "He had a tummy ache; why did you give him mesquite bark?" "That's all I had," she would whisper.

In stories about the tree, the bark, and faith, Eva links her "inner being" to historical narratives about "where we came from." [7] For this Day of the Dead celebration, Eva's emphasis on faith and family reinforces the importance of Mexican beliefs and rituals. Through

Eva creates altars for each room of her home and in other
places such as the "Youth on the Move" Center where this
altar is displayed. Under the lace Virgin of Guadalupe is a
ring of Eva's wax and paper flowers.

the metaphor of faith, she asserts the rights and regional identity of
Mexican Americans. From the nineteenth-century *vaqueros*, miners,
and mule-packers to the early twentieth-century railroad men to
today's growing group of agricultural workers, Mexicans have been
central to eastern Oregon's history. They know the land intimately,
even if ownership rests with the "master." The healer in the traditional tale can perform miracles, but so too can ordinary family
members. The miracles invoked here may be viewed as religious.
However, the story of the master also invites secular interpretation,
including a respect for nature and its bounty in the depiction of
her father praying to the trees and taking just what he needed. Her
father's actions reinforce the tree as embodiment of spiritual power,
a belief rooted in numerous indigenous cultures (cf. Mauzé 1998).

Here in a local arts center, Eva's verbal artistry is most evident. In
narrating stories within stories, she startles us into seeing an unexpected connection between healing, faith, and being Mexican.

Eva pointing to masks made by local young people
who come to her "Youth on the Move" program
housed in a trailer on the edge of Nyssa.

Nyssa, Oregon, September 2004

"How do you measure faith? How do you measure the child's first
words after silence, the coming back?" Eva asks me in a trailer at
the edge of Nyssa, directly across from the Amalgamated Sugar
Factory where many of her family members work. This is the home
of "Youth on the Move," a program for at-risk Latino youth, some
of whom are gang members. At the trailer, Eva is everyone's *Ipa*—
grandmother—teaching traditional Mexican arts such as her *coronas*, masks, and Day of the Dead altars.

Eva points to one chair and says, "There was a young woman,
fifteen years old, who sat in that chair for weeks, saying nothing.
Then, one day, a whisper: 'My daddy does things to me at night.' It
was so hard for her to say. But she could come here day after day,

just to have that chair to sit on, to wait. And you must wait with them. How do you know when a child will come to life?"

Eva grows frustrated with arts agencies that want measurements and statistics; her work is aimed at broader, unquantifiable trans-formation. I bear this in mind as we sit with a scrapbook of photos taken over the many years she has worked with local youth. Based on our conversation, I will write a report to an agency that has sup-ported Eva's work. Her goal is two-fold: to change young people's behavior and to change outsiders' perception of gang members and other troubled young people.

Eva tells me story after story of how learning Mexican arts and culture helps these young people "heal the root." Many times, the gang members have turned away from a fight, saying, "Our *Ipa* is with us." She trusts these adolescents, sometimes sending them to the store with her wallet, which is returned with her cash intact. Eva states, "I have never, ever, and this is from the bottom of my heart and knowledge of my life, I have never seen the people that the school describes or the police. I have never seen it. And I have had them together here, the blues and the reds [different gangs]." She aims to overturn a "public narrative" about young Latinos as dan-gerous and socially marginal, offering new, inverted interpretations of contemporary Latino life (Davis 2002:23). "Healing the root" reaches to the past as a resource for action and social change, but it is ultimately a script for the future.

Eva ends with the story emblematic of her Mexican heritage—healing with the mesquite bark—the legacy that can save these teenagers. The roots of culture may not be immediately visible, but using what is at hand—the bark—can begin the process of instilling faith. Eva returns to her mother's legacy:

> This is the way her daughter remembers her. I can remember thinking she was working miracles. How come with the little bark of mesquite tree that she sent me out to get? I'd say, "Mama, why did you give her mesquite bark?" "Because that's all I had." And the person was healed! So you see how far back it comes that it is in your heart what happens to you, too.
>
> Not only illness can overpower you. It is also yourself and your faith and whatever you know. Because the people had faith in her and she had faith in herself and in the bark. And she gave it and they were healed.

Eva's stories of faith evoke indigenous practices and arts as healing the psychic and social dislocation from one's "roots." Her family stories connect to broader political, historical, and cultural narratives. Though Eva is not a member of an organized group, her narratives are "social acts" linked to the Chicano movement (Davis 2002). Faith in tradition is more than mere nostalgia; rather, Eva's stories suggest a creative use of history to meet the demands of contemporary Latino life, especially for marginalized groups. Stories can be healing, but we enact faith through deeds, not by words alone. Metaphor is powerful in part because "we act according to the way we conceive of things" (Lakoff and Johnson 1980:5).

Conclusion

Every day, Eva faces something that would shake the faith of someone with less resolve—the pain and illness of those who come for healing, ongoing financial instability, the violent murder of a granddaughter, and most recently the loss of her possessions when her house burned down. The metaphors that surround immeasurable faith—the tree, its root, and bark—form the skeletal structure for her beliefs and teachings. Each story that branches from them is critical to her "equipment for living," sustaining narratives that she tells herself as well as others (Cruikshank 1998).

Metaphor helps us understand one domain of experience in terms of another (Lakoff and Johnson 1980). Faith is ephemeral, an abstraction that seeks concrete enactment through rituals and symbols. That Eva has maintained her faith through multiple hardships stands contrary to reason, but metaphor is the perfect vehicle for expressing such contradiction. Metaphor invites us to "turn our backs on reason" because "logically, two things can never be the same thing and still remain two things" (Frye 1964:32). The tree, its roots, and the healing bark form a series of interconnecting associations that make faith seem both logical and real for Eva's listeners. She also evokes faith through contrasts—its vastness implied by the inverse notions of measurement and weight, its malleability and adaptability set against the rigid, "too-tight dress" of institutional religion. Further, Eva uses metaphor to creatively improvise on a repertoire of stories that ground her personal experience in the context of Mexican culture and history. She shows us how personal stories are shaped by narrative conventions and how an individual storyteller reforms traditional tales. Similarly, her stories and practice as a *curandera* have a social dimension, revealing healing as a cultural response to oppression and a "reclaiming of memory as the remedy for rootlessness" (cf. Fernandez Olmos and Paravisini-Gebert 2001:xxi).

For Eva, an historical and cultural legacy is a source of power but not a confining straightjacket. As Briggs points out, "the past rather stands as a communicative resource, providing a setting and an expressive pattern for discussions that transform both past and present" (1988:99). Like other elements of stories, metaphors frame our understanding of a particular situation but also invite application to other contexts. This flexibility allows an audience multiple paths for interpretation, both secular and religious. Literary devices are far more than flourishes on Eva's narrative message, for "aesthetics is not merely ornament and appreciation; it is a form of knowledge" (Portelli 2001:x). Further, knowledge of the past may motivate action in the present. Eva's root metaphors can "catalyze thought" in listeners, while at the same time pointing toward key scenarios of "overt action in the public world" (Ortner 1973:1342).

Over time, Eva and I have moved from more formal interviews to ongoing conversations; my goal is a more collaborative and reciprocal ethnography (Lassiter 2005; Lawless 1993). Yet that reciprocity isn't always straightforward. When I asked Eva which of her teachings I should include in writing about her, she responded to the issue of teaching. "It wasn't like teaching. My mother didn't say, 'Sit down. I'm gonna teach you. . . . I watched!" Eva was telling me, it seemed, that I must learn by attention, observation, and trust. What is important cannot be directly related—the implicit invitation to metaphor. When I asked again what I should write, Eva said, "You decide, Jo. I trust you to know. I have faith."

Such dialogue cracks a window onto the relationship between ethnographers and our hosts and the ways we communicate (Cruikshank 1998:25). But as dialogue develops, so do potential challenges. Erika Friedl argues that the longer we work with someone, the greater our potential for developing "period eye," an art historical concept she adapts from Clifford Geertz. The sharper one's period eye, the more readily one can uncover layers of meaning. What follows is the fear "that the next story, the next event, will rattle one's hard-won understanding" (Friedl 2004:8).

As Eva's stories shift and expand in different contexts, my understanding often founders. The constancy of metaphors such as the tree and the root hearten me, offering a tool for interpreting Eva's narratives as well as the embedded lessons about faith and how to live. I suspect that metaphor functions similarly for Eva—a stable structure for generating new combinations of oral tradition and personal narrative, each responsive to different audiences.

Acknowledgments

I am grateful to Barbara Babcock, Elaine Lawless, Kirin Narayan, and Bill Schneider for insightful readings of this essay.

Notes

1. Lakoff and Johnson (1980:25) differentiate between ontological metaphors that help us to view "events, activities, emotions, ideas, etc. as entities and substances." Faith is evoked as beyond measure in contrast to the metaphor of the yardstick and the scale. It is, in this sense, a sort of "anti-entity" metaphor. In contrast, orientational metaphors such as the tree organize a system of concepts in relation to one another. The roots, bark, and trunk of the tree all evoke different aspects of culture.

2. For an overview of stories in interview contexts, see Narayan and George 2002. For an exploration of the relationship of oral and written versions of stories, see Morrow and Schneider 1995; for a focus on specific oral retellings, see Cruikshank 1998.

3. I am following the work of Hymes (1981) and Bauman (1977) in describing Eva's use of metaphor as artistic: that is, as part of a performative event in which language carries more than referential meaning, indicating to the listener to interpret what is said "in some special sense" (Bauman 1977:9).

4. The tree of life gained importance after the Mexican revolution when the government actively encouraged production of folk arts, spurring a century of collecting. Many collections included tree of life ceramics and candelabras. In the 1970s, fifty-two trees were placed in Mexican embassies throughout the world, marking the tree of life as a dominant symbol of Mexican culture. For a fuller discussion of the tree of life in Mexican art, see Lenore Hoag Mulryan 2004. For more on the symbolism of trees, see Porteous 2002 and Rival 1998.

5. Feminist scholars have chronicled the need for explicit attention to intersubjectivity, power relations, and issues of ethics and representation. (See Babcock 2005; Behar and Gordon 1995; Gluck and Patai 1991; Personal Narratives Group 1989). For an overview of major trends in feminist ethnography and its connections to postmodern approaches, see Lassiter (2005:48–75).

6. The number of indigenous people of Mexican descent living in Oregon is difficult to calculate; however, the Mexican Consulate confirms that groups include Mixtecs and Zapotecs from Oaxaca, Otomís from Hidalgo, Purépechas from Michoacán, and Nahuas from Hidalgo and Veracruz.

7. Rival points out that trees are "perfect natural models for genealogical connections" (1998:11).

References

Babcock, Barbara. 2005. Bloomers, Bingos, the Orange 914, and Helen's Dress: Stories from the Field that I Have to Tell You. *Anthropology and Humanism Quarterly* 30(2):171–78.

———. 1993. Shaping Selves, Shaping Lives: The Art and Experience of Helen Cordero. In *Imagery and Creativity: Ethnoaesthetics and Art Worlds in the Americas*. Dorothea S. Whitten and Norman E. Whitten, Jr., eds., 205–34. Tucson: University of Arizona Press, 1993.

Bauman, Richard. 1977. *Verbal Art as Performance*. Prospect Heights, IL: Waveland Press.

Becker, Gay. 1997. *Disrupted Lives: How People Create Meaning in a Chaotic World*. Berkeley: University of California Press.

Behar, Ruth, and Deborah Gordon, eds. 1995. *Women Writing Culture*. Berkeley: University of California Press.

Briggs, Charles. 1988. *Competence in Performance: The Creativity of Tradition in Mexicano Verbal Art*. Philadelphia: University of Pennsylvania Press.

Cruikshank, Julie. 1998. *The Social Life of Stories: Narrative and Knowledge in the Yukon Territory*. Lincoln: University of Nebraska Press.

Davis, Joseph E., ed. 2002. *Stories of Change: Narrative and Social Movements*. Albany: State University of New York Press.

Fenandez, James. 1974. The Mission of Metaphor in Expressive Culture. *Current Anthropology* 15(2): 119–45.

Fernandez Olmos, Margarite, and Lizabeth Paravisini-Gebert, eds. 2001. *Healing Cultures: Art and Religion as Curative Practices in the Caribbean and its Diaspora*. New York: Palgrave.

Friedl, Erika. 2004. Stories as Ethnographic Dilemma in Longitudinal Research. *Anthropology and Humanism Quarterly* 29(1):5–21.

Frye, Northrop. 1964. The Motive for Metaphor. In *The Educated Imagination*. Bloomington: Indiana University Press.

Gamboa, Erasmo. 1995. The Bracero Program in *Nosotros: The Hispanic People of Oregon: Essays and Reflections*. Erasmo Gamboa and Carolyn M. Buan, eds., 41–44. Portland: Oregon Council for the Humanities.

Gluck, Sherna Berger, and Daphne Patai. 1991. *Women's Words: The Feminist Practice of Oral History*. NY: Routledge.

Hymes, Dell. 1981. *In Vain I Tried to Tell You*. Philadelphia: University of Pennsylvania Press.

Lakoff, George, and Mark Johnson. 1980. *Metaphors We Live By*. Chicago: University of Chicago Press.

Lassiter, Luke Eric. 2005. *The Chicago Guide to Collaborative Ethnography*. Chicago: University of Chicago Press.

Lawless, Elaine. 1993. *Holy Women, Wholly Women: Sharing Ministries of Wholeness Through Life Histories and Reciprocal Ethnography*. Washington, D.C.: American Folklore Society, New Series.

Mauzé, Marie. 1998. Northwest Coast Trees: From Metaphors in Culture to Symbols of Culture. In *The Social Life of Trees: Anthropological Perspectives on Tree Symbolism*. Laura Rival, ed., 233–51. New York: Oxford University Press.

McCarthy Brown, Karen. 1991. *Mama Lola: A Vodou Priestess in Brooklyn.* Berkeley: University of California Press.

Morrow, Phyllis, and William Schneider, eds. 1995. *When Our Words Return: Writing, Hearing and Remembering Oral Traditions of Alaska and the Yukon.* Logan, Utah: Utah State University Press.

Mulcahy, Joanne. 2000. *Birth and Rebirth on an Alaskan Island.* Athens: University of Georgia Press.

Mulryan, Lenore Hoag. 2004. *Ceramic Trees of Life: Popular Art from Mexico.* Los Angeles: UCLA Fowler Museum.

Napoleon, Harold. 1991. *Yuuyaraq: The Way of the Human Being.* Eric Madsen, ed.. Fairbanks: Center for Cross-Cultural Studies, University of Alaska Fairbanks.

Narayan, Kirin. 1989. *Storytellers, Saints and Scoundrels.* Philadelphia: University of Pennsylvania Press.

Narayan, Kirin, and Kenneth M. George. 2002. Personal and Folk Narrative as Cultural Representation. *Handbook of Interview Research: Context and Method.* Gubrium, Jaber F. and James A. Holstein, eds., 815–31. Thousand Oaks: Sage.

Ortner, Sherry. 1973. On Key Symbols. *American Anthropologist* 75(5); 1328–46.

Personal Narratives Group, eds. 1989. *Interpreting Women's Lives: Feminist Theory and Personal Narratives.* Bloomington: Indiana University Press.

Portelli, Alessandro. 2001. *The Death of Luigi Trastulli and Other Stories.* Albany: State University of New York Press.

Porteous, Alexander. 2002. *The Forest in Folklore and Mythology.* Mineola, NY: Dover.

Rival, Laura, ed. 1998. *The Social Life of Trees: Anthropological Perspectives on Tree Symbolism.* New York: Oxford University Press.

Trotter, Robert T., II, and Juan Antonio Chavira. 1997. *Curanderismo: Mexican-American Folk Healing.* Athens: University of Georgia Press.

The Weight of Faith

Generative Metaphors in the Stories of Eva Castellanoz: A Conversation with Joanne B. Mulcahy and Barbara A. Babcock

Joanne Mulcahy and Barbara Babcock point out how Eva Castellanoz's stories are part of a cultural tradition that she shares with her ancestors—a bond that sustains knowledge through generations and nourishes the teller and her guests today. For Mulcahy and Babcock, metaphors help transcend cultural differences and provide a way to share their understandings, experiences, and feelings. The relationships formed in the process are too often left out of public discourse, too often dismissed as unimportant, despite the fact that the relationships are the reason and basis for sharing the stories.

BABCOCK: When I read about Eva and her stories, the first words that come to mind are Leslie Silko's stories about Pueblo stories and storytelling. The words I cannot forget come from the title poem in her novel *Ceremony* [1977], and from her essay, "Language and Literature from a Pueblo Indian Perspective," in *Yellow Woman and a Beauty of the Spirit* [1996] in which she describes stories as "life for the people," as essential to survival: "you don't have anything if you don't have stories;" as a way of "bringing us together, keeping this whole together, keeping this family together"—past, present,

---

Barbara A. Babcock is Regents Professor of English at the University of Arizona. She is known for her scholarship in folklore, literary theory, anthropology, and cultural studies. For sixteen years, she worked with Helen Cordero, a potter from Cochiti Pueblo and inventor of the now well known storyteller figures. In addition to *The Pueblo Storyteller: Development of a Figurative Ceramic Tradition* (1986), co-authored with Guy and Doris Monthan, Babcock has published numerous essays analyzing Cordero's work in terms of gender and cultural production, as well as reproduction, power, and other issues embodied in Pueblo "potteries" and the representation thereof. Her work also includes such edited collections as *The Reversible World: Symbolic Inversion in Art and Society* (1978); *Pueblo Mothers and Children: Essays by Elsie Clews Parsons, 1915–1924* (1991); and, with Marta Weigle, *The Great Southwest of the Fred Harvey Company and the Santa Fe Railway* (1996).

and yet unborn. Silko tells us, "when Aunt Susie told her stories, she would tell a younger child to go open the door so that our esteemed predecessors might bring their gifts to us. . . . 'Let them come in. They're here, they're here with us *within* the stories.'" And in Pueblo culture, the spider's web is, like the tree of life in Eva's stories, the root metaphor, the genealogical model. What both Leslie and Eva tell us, as Joanne points out, is that stories embody the individual as well as the cultural "generativity" and "chaining" that both folklorists and psychologists talk about.

MULCAHY: I appreciate how Barbara points out the critical dimension that stories play in all cultures: the ways "root" metaphors form a central core for meaning and reproduce culture through stories. Her comments also reminded me of how deceptively simple it can sound to say, as Silko does, "You don't have anything if you don't have the stories." The meaning of stories, how they are told and retold, is shaped very specifically to meet cultural needs. When Aunt Susie opened the door to let the ancestors bring their gifts, she revealed the different contours of the Pueblo universe. Similarly, when Eva tells me how her mother healed with the mesquite bark and her faith, I cannot collapse her narrative into one more familiar to me. Stories have their own integrity, but through metaphor— the spider's web; the tree and its root, bark, and branches—we can go beyond logic and inhabit, even briefly, a world different from our own.

BABCOCK: When I read Joanne and other women scholars working to tell the stories and the lives of other women, I am struck by the complexities of intersubjectivity; by the ways in which the spaces between women of different worlds, different cultures, different ages, etc. are mediated by stories; and by the ways in which both the relationships and the stories change and reshape each other over time. And then there is the story of the relationship itself which is very rarely told, which most of us were trained not to tell, or in cases like this, to regard as gossip, as "girl stuff," and this is probably the most important story of all.

MULCAHY: Yes, these are the levels of stories that are not deemed important enough to tell. For years, feminist scholars have worked to break down the distinctions between men's sanctioned, often public, stories and the less visible and frequently derided stories women tell. It's ironic that after nearly four decades of major feminist contributions, the relationship between feminist scholars and our subjects remains one of the last taboos: "girl's stuff," as Barbara says, is too embarrassing to discuss. This taboo crosses over into the realm of writing, genre, and our own academic storytelling. We need new literary forms as well as a voice to convey "intersubjectivity." I want to bring readers' attention to Barbara's recently published essay, "Bloomers, Bingos, the Orange 914, and Helen's Dress: Stories from the Field I Have to Tell You," in *Anthropology and Humanism Quarterly* [2005] that addresses these issues by telling personal stories. We need many more such leaps into creative experimentation.

BABCOCK: At the same time that I read Joanne's revised essay, I read Elena Poniatowski's wonderful introduction to *Here's to You, Jesusa!* [2001], which vividly captures this difficult yet increasingly indispensable business of women telling and writing the stories of other women. In addition to the aforementioned intersubjectivity, her description of Jesusa's reaction to the tape recorder, which she described as an "animal," and which Elena stopped using, made me realize that we probably need to say more than we have about both the circumstances of telling and the methods of recording. I could never, for example, walk into Helen's house and turn on a recorder or take photos. Whether or not there is an "animal" in the room obviously makes a difference.

MULCAHY: The "animal" in the house that Barbara references from her own fieldwork with Helen Cordero and from Poniatowski's story raised important questions for me. How much do we reveal about our fieldwork? For Eva, tape recorders and other devices are not an impediment; she has worked as a fieldworker for the Oregon and Idaho Folk Arts Programs. However, Barbara's questions raise another issue about our relationships with the people whose stories we're recording. Does the "animal" in the room detract from our focus on the two people who are working together? Do we neglect the interpersonal for the focus on "getting the story?" We need to record the process of our work as well as the story itself.

6

The Representation of Politics and the Politics of Representation

Historicizing Palestinian Women's Narratives

Sherna Berger Gluck

Sherna Gluck is an historian and founder of the
Virtual Oral/Aural History Archive at California
State University at Long Beach. She is an active
member of the Oral History Association and the
International Oral History Association. In this essay,
she describes her research on the role of women during the first Palestinian *intifada* and the evolution of
a Palestinian women's movement. Discovering that
the story differs with each telling, she questions how
the political climate at the time influences what gets
emphasized in any particular recounting of the past.

Introduction

As oral historians, we often admonish novices not to reinterview
people whose narratives have been recorded already; or if they
do, to read the previous oral histories and not to cover the same
ground. On the other hand, as we increasingly problematize oral
histories and analyze the various factors that shape narrators' representations, this advice might prove, instead, to be antihistorical.
Realizing that people's representations will change depending not
only on their own personal developments but also on the changing sociopolitical contexts in which the interview is conducted, can
we assume that a narrative is more than merely a very transitory

representation? On the other hand, if the same questions are explored at different periods of time with the same narrators, might we be in a better position to make these transitory representations more historically meaningful—or least, more comprehensible?

The high visibility of women during the first Palestinian *intifada* (1987–1993) attracted a host of feminist scholars and activists to the Occupied Palestinian Territories (OPT), many of whom recorded interviews with women leaders.[1] Most of the narratives collected in this period, like those recorded before the *intifada*, were primarily with urban activists and intellectuals—and frequently were with the same people. So, too, are the memoirs subsequently written by Palestinian women.[2] The origin story of the contemporary women's movement figures prominently in these narratives and served as the basis for a general consensus that the women's committees—or at least their leadership—to varying degrees came to embrace feminism in the course of the *intifada*. Was this, indeed, a transformation in their consciousness? An exploration of the "retellings" of their movement's history and activism, including a discussion of the development of their feminist consciousness, provides an opportunity to consider how the changing political context might have shaped the production of their narratives.

To explore the varying representations of political events and consciousness, as well as the way that the shifting political situation influenced these representations, I will draw on a host of these different narratives. These include my own repeated interviews collected over a period of almost six years (1989–94); the 1985–86 interviews conducted by Orayb Najjar, the 1985 interviews conducted by Joost Hilterman, and the 1995 interviews conducted by Frances Hasso with both men and women of the Democratic Front for the Liberation of Palestine (DFLP). An unpublished 1993 memoir of Fadwa al-Labadi, a former DFLP cadre is also very revealing (al-Labadi 1993). Unfortunately, most of these other interviews were not available at the time I began my work, or the identity of the narrators was disguised—an argument, I suppose, against anonymity.[3] To understand the various contexts in which the "retellings" occurred, it is critical to understand the political developments in the Palestinian national movement and women's historic roles.

Palestinian Nationalism and Women's Historic Roles

December 9, 1987, marks the beginning of what is now identified as the first *intifada*, the popular uprising against Israeli occupation of the West Bank, including East Jerusalem, and Gaza. It was sparked by an auto accident in Jabalya refugee camp outside of Gaza City in which an Israeli driver struck and injured four Palestinians. Initially local, over the next several weeks, actions against the Israeli occupation spread to the West Bank, and eventually the entire Palestinian population in the Occupied Palestinian Territories (OPT) was mobilized into a largely nonviolent, mass popular movement (Gluck 1994). The television images of older women in traditional clothing engaged in street demonstrations, including stone throwing, was the more public face of women's role to the outside world. Behind the walls, however, their role was even more critical. Among other activities, they organized underground classes when the schools were closed, monitored their neighborhoods to ensure that all families were getting adequate nutrition, developed small-scale economic projects, and worked with the various committees that had been formed to establish health clinics.

Women's organized nationalist activities were not new. They date back to 1921 when the Palestinian Women's Union was organized to improve the standards of living of the poor and organize women around national activities. Six years later, during the convening of the First Arab Women's Congress in Jerusalem, delegates met with the British High Commissioner to protest Zionist immigration and the Balfour Declaration.[4] Women also played critical—but often invisible—support roles during the 1936–39 revolt against British rule. During the Arab-Israeli war in 1948–49 following Israel's declaration of independence, and again in 1967 during the Israeli invasion of the West Bank and Gaza, they provided invaluable assistance to the fleeing Palestinian refugees.

Although these earlier activities of women's volunteer organizations were confined largely to women of the elite, they did lay a foundation for women's activism. In fact, women of the earlier generation, particularly those who formed organizations to support the refugees in 1948, provided the training ground for many of the leaders of the later Palestinian women's movement. These contemporary leaders were part of the new generation of young Palestinian university students who had been raised under Israeli occupation. Their activism, which was initially spurred by nationalism and class consciousness, ultimately fomented a nascent feminist consciousness. Consequently, although the many of the activities during the first *intifada* were designed primarily to help sustain the largely nonviolent uprising against Israeli occupation,

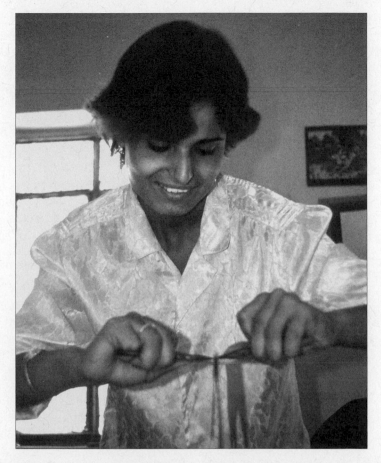

Women's Action Committee ceramic workshop, Issawiyeh, 1989.

they took on a life of their own and became an avenue for women's empowerment. This was particularly the case for the women's economic cooperatives that were formed in the countryside and refugee camps.

Origin Stories

To explore the varying representations of feminist consciousness, we must look at the ways that political affiliation, generation, and the dating of a narrative influence historical rendition. Regardless of their political affiliation or ideological bent, it is significant that all women activists begin their origin story with the 1978 formation of the Working Women's Committee. And of those who were in the Occupied Palestinian Territories at the time—and out of jail—*all* claim to have attended the founding meeting. The accounts of two leading Democratic Front (DFLP) party cadres recorded in the 1980s sound remarkably similar. For instance, in 1985, Siham Barghouti explained:

> We began to suspect that we were following the wrong approach by having mixed work parties [in the Voluntary Work Committees], and we needed to work only with women. So we tried to work with existing women's organizations. . . . but we felt uneasy about the way traditional women's societies function. . . . We felt that there was a need for a more broad-based women's organization, with no age limit, one in which decisions were not formulated from the top down. . . . We published an open letter inviting women to join us. Between fifteen to twenty women responded on March 8, 1978, and the Women's Work [Committees] . . . was born. (Najjar 1992:127).

Except for a difference in head counts, Zahera Kamal's description four years later did not stray far from Barghouti's:

> Many of us, we were in charitable societies. . . . We had a discussion . . . about twenty-five or thirty women . . . we had an idea that this is the work we should [be doing]. We have to change the role of woman in the society, and if we want to do that, we should have other kinds of work. . . . And in 1978 we started a committee . . . that could have all the women . . . it wasn't concerned with just one party.[5]

Not surprisingly, for security reasons, neither Kamal nor Barghouti discuss their membership in the Democratic Front (DFLP) and the central role that DFLP women cadres played in the formation of the committee, though Barghouti does hint at a vague "organizational we." And even though Kamal and Barghouti both imply that the women themselves were the force behind the process, there is an emotional flatness in their accounts, in sharp contrast to each of their descriptions of their own very early feminist awakenings.[6] By contrast, Fadwa al-Labadi, their DFLP contemporary who penned her memoirs in 1993 after a rather ugly split in the party, was more willing to open old wounds and to expose the extent to which the male DFLP leadership was the force behind the organizing of the first women's committee:

> In 1977, we [the women members of the Voluntary Work Committee (VWC)] saw the need to involve more women in our group, especially from the poorer segments of society. Soon we became active in trying to mobilize women. The main aim was to take part in the national struggle . . . [and we] could also raise the consciousness of their situation in

A demonstration of women activists, 1991.

society that discriminated against them. . . . Our leaders [in the DFLP]
told women members to mobilize into the VWC and then to recruit
them into the political party. . . . The reason that most of the women
were reluctant to join the VWC was because it had mixed membership. . . . We discussed this issue with our leaders, who redirected us to
cooperate with the women's charitable societies. . . .

We wanted a radically new approach to working among women—an
approach geared to development rather than to charity, to empowerment rather than dependency. (al-Labadi 1993:49)

Ten years after her interview quoted earlier, and after the split
in the party, Barghouti was also more willing to name the DFLP as
the organizational "we" to which she had alluded earlier.[7] Labadi
goes further, not only exposing the central, manipulative role of
the male leadership but also pointing to the fact that the women's
and men's agendas differed:

Many left-wing male members opposed our new establishment and
accused us of separatism; their justification was that mixed organizations
are the best for women's emancipation. In reality they wanted women to
continue to be subjected to male domination. (Hasso 1997:50)

The downplaying of their own feminist agenda by the older, then-loyal DFLP party members contrasts with a younger cohort who also attended the founding meeting. Regardless of their differing political affiliations, these younger activists describe coming to the group in terms that reflected a dawning feminist consciousness, no matter how it was labeled at the time. At the very least, as one activist from Hebron suggested in a 1985 interview, it was a way of claiming space for a new generation of women activists (Hilterman 1985:132).

To Be or Not To Be: Representations of Feminist Consciousness

It is not surprising to hear differing accounts of the same event from different participants and, indeed, different ascriptions of meaning. And we are certainly accustomed to narrators engaging in less subterfuge as their political loyalties shift. Multiple interviews done over a ten-year period with the same set of women leaders makes it possible to go even further and to explore how the changing political climate, rather than just an individual's changing political alliances, shaped their representations of feminist consciousness.

Initially relying on our own interviews done over the course of the *intifada*, observers of the women's movement from both inside and outside the OPT, and quite independent of each other, reached an early consensus about the evolving feminist commitment of the various women's committees—or at least what was perceived as a growing tendency not to privilege nationalism over feminism. I certainly drew that conclusion, for instance, from the repeat interviews that I conducted from early 1989 to mid-1994 with Maha Nassar, the leader of the Union of Palestinian Women's Committees (UPWC)—the committee that other local activists viewed as the most resistant to embracing feminism (see, for instance, Strum 1992:219).

Indeed, by the time we conversed in 1991, Nassar's unhesitant espousal of feminism seemed a far cry from our first interview in January 1989. Then, the tension created by trying to toe the nationalist line while simultaneously espousing women's liberation yielded a rather ambivalent and equivocal response when I asked if her organization could be considered feminist:

> We are women liberation movements. . . . We believe that our liberation cannot be achieved fully unless our society is liberated. . . . The most oppressed sector of the society are women. That's why it doesn't mean that we have to stop our liberation for ourselves until the liberation for

Union of Palestinian Women's Committees canning project, Saer, 1991.

the society is achieved. It means that we will have to go on both sides; to make our activities . . . all together to make—our nation. To end occupation and to have our independent state.[8]

The change from this interview to my final meeting with Nassar in 1994 seemed complete and was reinforced by the barrage of excited phone calls she was receiving during our visit about her rumored establishment of a woman's shelter in her home.

Using the early *intifada* years as our starting point, and comparing the narratives collected from the 1987–89 period with those of the later years, our initial conclusions about a transformation in feminist consciousness seemed warranted. However, going back to even earlier narratives that eventually became available and taking a closer historical reading, this conclusion becomes suspect.

Kufr Nameh village activists, 1991.

Instead, we see that women's issues, which are viewed as potentially divisive, are more severely circumscribed when there is greater pressure for political unity and especially for inter- and intrafactional national unity. For example, the period of the *intifada*, which Ted Swedenburg (1995) characterizes as one of national conformism, stands in sharp contrast to 1985, when the rapprochement among the various factions of the PLO had not been realized. This earlier pre-*intifada* period happens to be precisely when Joost Hiltermann conducted his interviews with women activists, in which an unnamed leader of the UPWC (who I could later identify as Maha Nassar) definitively proclaimed:

> We place the women's question before the national question. We focus all our activities on bringing the women out of their homes to make them more self-confident and independent. Once they believe in themselves, they will know that they can become leaders in any field they choose, including the military field. (Hilterman 1991:168)

It is a mistake, too, to view the *intifada* years as if they represented a coherent, undifferentiated era. Rather, there were shifts between what Arturo Escobar, in speaking of Latin America, refers to as the logic of "popular" struggle and the logic of "democratic" struggle (1992:40). The former is characterized by a unified political space, whereas the latter flowers in a plural space—exactly the kind of space that frees women to subscribe to antipatriarchal politics.

By 1991, with the beginning of U.S. shuttle diplomacy, and especially by 1994 with the establishment of the Palestinian Authority, the fragile national unity that characterized the earlier "popular struggle" period of the *intifada* broke down and the pressure for national conformism dissipated. Consequently, the leaders of the oppositionist Popular Front for the Liberation of Palestine (PFLP)-aligned UPWC shifted their discourse. Where they had been rather equivocal in their early *intifada* narratives, in this later period they once again became more willing to espouse feminism openly and to be self-critical of the way they had privileged the nationalist struggle. While issues like wife battering and sexual abuse (including incest) might have been addressed privately and secretly earlier, they were being brought to the surface and made public. A study by the Women's Studies Division of the Bisan Centre that revealed an unexpected high rate of incest helped to spur these discussions. Three years later, when I visited with Maha Nassar, she was at the center of a firestorm in the local community for having given refuge to a young woman attempting to flee a forced marriage.

The increasingly self-critical discourse of women's movement leaders, coupled with the loss of funds to maintain most of the grassroots projects that had empowered ordinary women, led some observers to reverse their earlier optimistic assessments. Instead, they concluded that the situation for women had worsened; that the space opened up during the *intifada* had proved to be fruitless. And although my closer reading and greater contextualization of the narratives of urban intellectual and political women has forced me, too, to reassess the impact of the *intifada*, we must take care not to render invisible the experiences of grassroots activists in villages and camps. My repeated interviews with them reveal how the "free space" opened during the early days of the *intifada* helped to spawn a feminist consciousness among them as well—even though this space may have closed in the post-*intifada* years (Gluck 1994, 1990).

Furthermore, the assessment of either "regression" in feminist consciousness or the earlier "progression" fails to acknowledge how the fluctuations in the unity of the national movement variously impacted women's ability to negotiate the terrain—what I have alluded to elsewhere as being like shifting sands (Gluck 1997). In other words, when the various narratives are historicized, it becomes evident that there was not a change in the feminist consciousness of women's committee leaders. Rather, their ability to maneuver and act on this consciousness was sometimes more constrained than at other times, depending on the moment of the national struggle and the extent of unity. This in turn determined how they *represented* their consciousness at different historical moments over this ten-year time span.

Reflections on the Post-*Intifada* (One) Feminism–Nationalism Conundrum

By 1994, following the return of Yasir Arafat (Abu Amar) and Palestine Liberation Organization (PLO) leaders from exile, the first *intifada* was all but dead. The popular mass mobilization that had spawned a more participatory process and created a more open political environment was replaced with a return of a bureaucratic and patriarchal political climate and structure. Feminists eventually labeled this the rule of the *abus*, referring to the older patriarchal leaders who had all adopted *noms de guerre* with the Abu designation.[9] Although the PLO leaders from Tunisia and their contingent of police and soldiers were initially welcomed with open arms by much of the population, the honeymoon did not last. The long-standing simmering struggle for power between the "inside" (those in the OPT) and the "outside" (the exiled leaders in Tunisia)—and particularly between a new generation of leaders inside who had cut their eye teeth during the *intifada*—surfaced very quickly. To mobilize support, Arafat relied on the old clan structure, thus reinforcing the patriarchal basis of the society that had been undermined during the first *intifada*. As a result, instead of mobilizing support for the newly formed Palestinian Authority, Arafat and his loyalists from the outside fostered widespread opposition among the democratic forces that had developed inside the OPT. Their active challenges revived the kind of open spaces created during the *intifada* and fostered the rejuvenation of feminist organizing (Gluck 1995). It also led to a great deal of discussion and self-criticism of having given primacy to nationalism over feminism (Kuttab 1999). Even women who were formerly Fateh and Arafat loyalists agreed and joined with the opposition voices—at least on a women's agenda. Indeed, women mobilized across political factions when full equality was not guaranteed on the first draft of the Basic Law (the temporary constitution) issued in late 1993. Although their unified challenges led to improvements in the third draft, it was still not fully satisfactory.

While the women's movement leaders of the *intifada* days persisted in fighting for a women's agenda, joined by a new generation of women activists, the shift away from grassroots organizing that I had observed by 1994 became definitive. Instead, the phenomena identified as the "NGO-ization" of the women's movement led to increasingly specialized and professional work which, by and large, reflected the agendas of the donor agencies (Jad 2003; Kuttab 2006). Even the language shifted: gender consciousness was becoming the coin of the realm in the NGO world.

One can only surmise how the women's movement leaders of the first *intifada* would represent their feminist history and consciousness in a retelling today, and even what terminology they might use. Would the open spaces created by opposition to the rule of the *abus* promote a representation of a greater feminist consciousness and an unwillingness to subsume it under the nationalist struggle? Or will the recent (2006) victory of the Islamic forces in the Palestinian elections, along with renewed attacks by Israel, create a pressure for women to downplay their feminism and promote the primacy of nationalism and secular unity? However these new retellings might be framed, they can only be understood by grasping the dynamics of the new social and political developments.

Notes

1. All references to the *intifada* in this paper refer to what subsequently has to be viewed as the first *intifada*. A second *intifada* started in 2000 following the visit by Ariel Sharon to Haram Al Sharif (known in English as the Dome of the Rock).

2. Interviews from the *intifada* period are included in a host of articles and books, cited below. I am endebted to Frances Hasso who so generously gave me access to some of her interviews. The earlier interviews conducted by Joost Hilterman (1985) provided a basis for comparative analysis of the *pre-intifada* and *intifada* representations of feminist consciousness. These were quoted extensively in his doctoral dissertation, later published under the title *Behind the Intifada* (1991). Finally, Orayb Najjar's early interviews were published later in her book, *Portraits of Palestinian Women* (1992).

3. These interviews were conducted as early as 1985 but did not become available until they were published later. Although I was able to later identify some of the anonymous narrators, I did not have a basis for these judgements in the earlier phases of my research.
4. This refers to the declaration by Lord Balfour in 1917 of British support "for the establishment in Palestine of a national home for the Jewish people."
5. Interview conducted by Sherna Berger Gluck, January 1989.
6. For Kamal's background, see Sherna Berger Gluck (1994); the most detailed published account of Barghouti's early years can be found in Najjar's *Portraits of Palestinian Women* (1992).
7. See Frances Hasso's "Paradoxes of Gender/Politics: Nationalism, Feminism and Modernity in Contemporary Palestine" (1997), esp. chapters 3–4. Her dissertation research was recently published as *Resistance, Repression and Gender Politics in Occupied Palestine and Jordan* (2005).
8. Gluck interview, January 1989, Tape IA2–3.
9. *Abu* literally means father and was a traditional naming convention, with both men and women both being named for their first son; *Umm* for the mother and *Abu* for the father, e.g., Abu Khaled, Umm Khaled. The older generation of PLO leaders adopted *noms de guerre* using the designation of Abu, though the name they chose to accompany it was more symbolic, e.g. Abu Jihad. Yasir Arafat was known as Abu Amar.

References

Al-Labadi, Fadwa. 1993. Memoirs of a Palestinian Daughter. M.A. Thesis, University of Kent.

Escobar, Arturo. 1992. Imagining a Post-Development:Critical Thought, Development and Social Movements. *Social Text* 31(2):40.

Gluck, Sherna Berger. 1990. *We will not be Another Algeria: Women's Mass Organizations. Changing Consciousness and the Potential for Wome's Liberation in a future Palestinian State.* International Annual of Oral History. New York: Greenwood Press.

———. 1994. *An American Feminist in Palestine: The Intifada Years.* Philadelphia: Temple University Press.

———. 1995. Gender Politics and Nationalism. *Journal of Palestine Studies* 24(3):5–15.

———. 1997. Shifting Sands: The Feminist Nationalist Connection in the Palestinian movement. In *Feminist Nationalism.* Lois West, ed. New York: Routledge.

Hamami, Rima, and Eileen Kuttab. 1999. The Palestinian Women's Movement: Strategies towards Freedom and Democracy. *News from Within* 15(4):3–9.

Hasso, Frances. 1997. Paradoxes of Gender/Politics: Nationalism, Feminism, and Modernity in Contemporary Palestine. Ph.D. dissertation, University of Michigan.

———. 2005. *Resistance, Repression and Gender Politics in Occupied Palestine and Jordan.* Syracuse, NY: Syracuse University Press.

Hilterman, Joost. 1991. *Behind the Intifada.* Princeton: Princeton
University Press.
Jad, Islah. 2003. The NGOization of the Arab Women's Movement.
Al-Raida (English edition) 20(100):38–47.
Kuttab, Eileen. 2006. New Challenges for the Palestinian Women's
Movement. *This Week in Palestine* (internet monthly), #96, April.
Najjar, Orayb. 1992. *Portraits of Palestinian Women.* Salt Lake City:
University of Utah Press.
Strum, Philippa. 1992. *The Women are Marching.* Brooklyn: Lawrence Hill.
Swedenburg, Ted. 1995. *Memories of Revolt.* Minneapolis: University of
Minnesota Press.

The Representation of Politics and the Politics of Representation

A Conversation with Sherna Berger Gluck and Ted Swedenburg

Sherna Gluck and Ted Swedenburg, both knowledgeable about Palestinian history and politics, share their observations about how the political climate in Palestine influences the stories that are told. Their discussion leads us to consider the tension between the "official narratives" that are promulgated to serve a cause and the personal accounts that an individual may choose to share over time. In a similar way to the Crowell-Clifford discussion, we are asked to examine how the individual is influenced by the master narrative and the openings they find to express their version of a story, a version that may provide insight on influences affecting their lives.

SCHNEIDER: I'd like to start this discussion by having us go back to the two quotes Sherna gave from interviews with Maha Nassar and her reference to an extended conversation with Nassar in 1994. As I understand the differences between the three sessions: in the first, 1985, Nassar is saying that the woman's question has to be solved before there can be any solution at a society level. In 1989, she is saying that as women we cannot be liberated until our society is liberated, and then, in 1994, she is more explicit in indicting the prevalence of sexism and its effects on women.

GLUCK: It's significant, too, that she wasn't just talking to me in less equivocal terms. She clearly had become quite open and public in addressing taboo subjects like forced marriage and wife battering. That's why she was getting phone calls "accusing" her of opening a shelter for women.

Ted Swedenburg is a cultural anthropologist at the University of Arkansas. He is an expert on the Middle East, but his interests also extend to musical expression, popular culture, and issues of domination and resistance. His publication *Memories of Revolt: The 1936–1939 Rebellion and the Palestinian National Past* (1995) is referenced in Gluck's essay.

SCHNEIDER: So all three narratives can be true, even at all points in time, but the speaker chooses to emphasize one thing at one point in time and to place the emphasis differently at another point in time. Sherna, you have noted two dynamics operating here that influence how the story is told. I think we should explore (1) how the political climate can change the narrative and (2) how the evolution of a relationship with the narrator can influence what is shared.

GLUCK: In 1989, when I first interviewed the leadership of the various women's committees, the mass mobilization of the *intifada* was still in full swing and there was a great deal of coordination and communication among the various factions and their women's committees. Yet each of the factions guarded solidarity within their ranks and worked hard to woo new members. The progressive (leftist) women's committees played a central role in this process and also curried favor with the Western feminists who were visiting Palestine in order to gain their support for the *intifada*.

At the same time, however, they also resented what they perceived as Western feminist pressure on them to espouse feminism. I believe that this produced the kind of equivocation that was evident in the 1989 interview with Maha Nassar. It also marked conversations with other women leaders in her committee who argued for the primacy of the nationalist struggle.

By 1993–94, when I made my fifth return visit to Palestine, the shift away from nationalist unity and conformism was well underway and the women were themselves concerned about how their agenda was being undermined. At the same time, my five years of repeated visits and conversations with the women's committee's leaders led to greater trust and a more nuanced mutual understanding of the multiple forms of feminism—what I like to refer to as feminism in an effort to challenge the hegemonic Western definition. Nevertheless, I doubt that would have mattered had the political climate not shifted.

SWEDENBURG: I would also add that Sherna's 1994 conversation with Maha Nassar occurred during a time when Palestinians in the West Bank and Gaza, what was to become the Palestinian National Authority, were involved in what we might term state-building or proto-state building. The mass mobilizations led by the various political factions were over, and a different sort of national imperative was on the agenda. The atmosphere (in this era mislabeled in the West as the "peace process") created certain openings and made the espousal of feminist views much more respectable. In other words, what was on the agenda from 1994 to 1999 was building state structures, building an infrastructure, rather than the national liberation struggle. This contrasts with the earlier period of the national liberation struggle with its strong emphasis on national unity that discouraged articulations of "divisive" issues.

SCHNEIDER: Okay, so we are talking about some pretty strong political and social forces that can influence the way people express the story.

SWEDENBURG: Yes, and I'm very interested in the power of official narratives and their ability to marginalize and even remake popular memories. An interesting example is presented in H. Bruce Franklin's book *Vietnam and Other American Myths* [2001]. He discusses the very prominent and militant role played by GIs in the movement against war in Vietnam. This critical aspect of the anti-war movement—documented in the new film *Sir! No Sir!*—has been mostly forgotten, largely due to a concerted effort on the part of the U.S. agencies of public meaning to create a very different "memory" of the relationship between the peace movement and the GIs. This official, preferred memory is encapsulated in the obsessively repeated story of soldiers who were spat upon by peaceniks when they disembarked at the airport upon their return from Vietnam. Hollywood movies like the Rambo films played a major role in creating and sustaining such a memory. Franklin shows that this pervasive story is a myth, because no GIs returning from Vietnam landed at civilian airports. Yet so powerful is the force of this myth that a number of GIs actually "remember" being spat upon at the airport by antiwar demonstrators upon their return.

SCHNEIDER: Of course, in our discussion of the feminist role in the Palestinian struggle, we are not dealing with a static story about an event in time but an evolving narrative where, as Sherna points out, there are "shifts in the political climate" and "opening of spaces" for new forms of expression about the role of feminism in the Palestinian struggle.

GLUCK: This discussion reminds me of an experience I had in my early work. As you know, Will, my work in U.S. women's social history began with a focus on labor movement activists. I had done rather extensive interviews with Sarah Rozner, a rank-and-file organizer in the Amalgamated Clothing Workers of America (ACWA—now joined with the ILGWU in a single union, UNITE). Together with one of the paid staff of the union, Rozner had spearheaded the formation of a Women's Local (275) in Chicago. Women in other cities followed suit, and together they began to push for a Women's Bureau in the national union.

This period in the late 1920s was marked by internal strife in the union, and the women's efforts were defeated at the national convention, where the male leadership argued that this "separatism" would undermine the union. At the time, Mamie Santora was the only woman on the national Executive Board. The written record of the convention where the women's locals pushed their agenda seemed to indicate that Santora supported the male leadership's squelching of this effort. When I first interviewed Santora in 1975, she claimed that she agreed with and supported the position of the male leadership. However, when I went back and interviewed her again a few years later and returned to this discussion, she "spilled the beans," as it were. Indeed, she told me that she believed the women were right and that she had supported their effort in the deliberations. Her earlier telling was shaped by her belief that she thought that I was sent by the union.

The important point here is that if I hadn't returned and she had not retold the story, the record would have reflected her collaboration with the men rather than her support of the women— albeit behind the scenes. So, as critical as the political shifts are in opening spaces for espousing a range of often-divergent views, this garment worker illustration highlights how a growing relationship with a narrator also influences the narrative. Of course, this is always within a political climate—sometimes a very charged climate. In fact, the political context and the historical moment are part and parcel of the personal relationship and it is hard to extricate one from the other. In my work with and on Palestinian women, that relationship is perhaps more complicated, in contrast to the obvious influence of union politics in the case of the garment worker story.

7

Performance/Participation

A Museum Case Study in Participatory Theater

Lorraine McConaghy

Lorraine McConaghy is staff historian at Seattle's
Museum of History & Industry and is active in
regional and national public history associations. In
this essay, she introduces us to a readers' theatre project that engages visitors to the museum with the oral
history of Seattle and the Pacific Northwest. Unlike
the other authors in this volume, McConaghy stages
retellings as a way to present and preserve historical
experiences. She chooses the stories of people who
are not well recognized by the public and gives guests
to the museum a chance to read transcripts of the
interviews. Despite the passage of time, the cultural
divides, and the lack of familiarity with the individuals, she finds that readers identify with the stories
and the experiences of the characters. She main-
tains that respeaking spoken words offers program
participants the chance to slip into another persona
and encourages the emotional engagement that
precedes, contextualizes, and encourages learning.

Over the last twenty years, the oral history collection at Seattle's
Museum of History & Industry has undergone dramatic change.
Originally, oral history interviews were gathered as research mate-
rial to support the development of specific exhibitions, stored away

at the exhibition's conclusion, and inaccessible to the public. Then, the museum collected interviews that documented the achievements of Seattle's elite, as acts of respect and to encourage financial support of the museum. But over the last decade, the *Speaking of Seattle* oral history project has mounted an intentional effort to gather stories that first document the workplace experiences and perspectives of a diverse community and second provide balance to the elite experience and perspective that are well documented by the museum's other collections. Third and most recently, we have experimented with ways to bring these stories into the galleries, not just as recordings for visitors to listen to but as scripted programs in which gallery visitors re-voice the stories of others and are then encouraged to relate their experiences through their own stories.

Today, the *Speaking of Seattle* oral history interviews are incorporated into the library collection and made available to the museum staff and the public for research purposes. But beyond the standard oral history archiving and research function, in the last five years the museum has also developed a set of readers' theater scripts drawn from the oral history collection. In a very positive way, readers' theater has effectively claimed public space for these personal narratives and given them new life in each new retelling. The dramatization of personal experience has translated from professional performance to visitor participation, as we have shifted the presentation of readers' scripts from the stage to the gallery, from actors to visitors. This radical transfer of perspective and authority has offered ordinary people the opportunity to emerge from the audience and engage with the material as performers. As our visitors have participated in readers' theaters in the museum galleries, they have seamlessly role-played other experiences and other personae, giving their own voice to the provocative stories of other men and women. Immersed in these stories, our passive visitors have become active participants, using the power of the spoken word to share another's past experiences with an audience who then in turn become performers and relate oral history to their own lives.

This form of direct engagement with the past is revelatory and disorienting: imagine an African American man speaking the role of a white female Amtrak clerk, or a Japanese American teenaged girl speaking the role of a male African American welder. We often say that a museum is a safe place to explore unsafe ideas; the participatory readers' theater exploration of unsafe ideas is deeply experiential but safely abstracted by dramatized expression and

We all felt a kind
of kin because
we were black,
we were all
subject to the
same attitudes,
the same
treatment.

Photo Howard Giske/Museum of History & Industry

Readers present *Speaking Out!*, a readers' theater script largely based on oral history interviews, developed by the Black Heritage Society of Washington State and Seattle's Museum of History & Industry.

stylized interactions among readers. The script sets the rules. For a few moments, a museum visitor speaks a different memory than her own, stands in shoes other than her own, internalizes a different Seattle experience than her own, and then externalizes that experience with her own voice. The "I" shifts from the individual to the other, to the others, through the freeing medium of theater. These experiences and points of view are often painful and dangerous, speaking from the heart of a troubling past that one cannot venerate or romanticize.

The testimony of oral history offers dissenting voices to a comfortable narrative of Seattle's untroubled past. When the Seattle and King County Historical Society organized in 1911, the founders were largely the descendants of the city's first American settlers, prominent and well-to-do. They hoped to perpetuate and enshrine a heroic mythology of Seattle's past. Their merged personal collections of family memorabilia became the core of the society's collection, which continued to grow under the founders' vision, privileging elite costumes, artifacts, scrapbooks, and journals. In effect, the entire collection became celebratory of a founding and building legend—a set of trophies, icons, and hagiographic relics to illustrate a story of success.

After World War II, the trustees devoted tremendous energy to opening a history museum in Seattle, named the Museum of

History & Industry. With this proposed title, the trustees intentionally courted the city's industrialists, entrepreneurs, and businessmen, joining well-heeled newcomers with the distinguished descendants of old-timers. In the proposed museum, the heroic story of pioneer progress embraced twentieth-century heroes, too. The historical society's story of industrial innovation and success comprised a comforting civic narrative of progress, self-satisfied and optimistic; indeed, it was that onward-and-upward story that the founders of the museum promised their supporters they would celebrate. This strategy successfully fulfilled the historical society's midcentury fundraising.

By the museum's opening in 1952, the collection richly supported stories of pioneer heroism, industrial progress, and elite success. There were many examples of elaborate wedding dresses and Parisian haute couture but no housedresses or riveters' overalls. Many examples of industrial products but not the tools that made them. Many examples of elaborate dinner settings and shining silver tea sets but no humble tableware. And on and on. And, like it or not, a museum's collection determines the stories told in its galleries. Curators have a powerful responsibility to the existing collection of artifacts, and museum visitors expect to see those artifacts, believing that the museum's authority springs from the collection's authenticity. At the Museum of History & Industry, curatorial work became connoisseurship, and rarely was an artifact presented in an interpretation that told all of its stories as a socially constructed object. For instance, an elegantly embroidered tablecloth might have been used as a point of departure to explore the lives of the Swedish piecework needleworker who sewed it, the Chinese laundryworker who washed it, the Irish housemaid who ironed it, and the Black cook who made the dinner—as well as the society hostess who decorated her table with it. But our collection didn't include those other stories.

The museum's history exhibitions became fables about the bravery of pioneers, the just rewards of honest toil, and the inevitability of progress, illustrated from the collection. There was a time when one could visit the Museum of History & Industry galleries and learn nothing about native history, economic history, labor history, the histories of people of color, women's history, or environmental history. During the 1960s, the museum's most influential trustee barred inclusion of Seattle's labor history in the galleries. The museum's longtime director refused to allow mention of Seattle's

Japanese internment in museum exhibits; the traveling exhibition
Pride and Shame was shown in 1970 while she was on vacation.
Seattle's real histories were perceived dimly, as a pallid backdrop
for vivid corporate and personal biographies presented as morality tales. But this didactic narrative was inaccurate, incomplete,
and unsatisfying. What was really missing in the galleries were the
ordinary people whose experiences could bring honesty and reality to the story, whose experiences could make the history in the
museum's galleries make sense. Museum visitors knew that Seattle's
history wasn't just about silver tea services and embroidered table-
cloths, signing business deals and building skyscrapers. By 1975,
the Museum of History & Industry was known as an elitist institution, speaking from its collection to a smaller and smaller slice of
Seattle's museum-going public.

Changing a collecting policy is an act not undertaken lightly; it
has dramatic consequences far into the future. But the Museum
of History & Industry has changed its policy; for more than twenty
years, the museum has no longer collected only the correspon-
dence, dining tables, and sable capes of the rich and famous and
has aggressively sought to diversify what it does collect. Future
museum curators and historians will be grateful for the sea-change
that is well underway. But little can be done to redress sins of omis-
sion in the past. Many opportunities to collect the material culture
of ordinary people have gone, never to return. The housedresses
and overalls are worn out and thrown away; the tableware broken
and the tools forgotten. Fortunately and in the nick of time, oral
history offers a slender bridge to that lost everyday past, to the stories that contexted those artifacts.

The museum's earliest oral history interviews were conducted in
the 1970s and 1980s to support specific exhibit research, and also
with the city's movers and shakers. These interviews with prominent industrialists, businessmen, and politicians were often wide-
ranging and interesting, but they suggested to a new generation
of curators a means of accessing different narratives of Seattle's
history. In fact, oral history offered an explicit, intentional strategy
to broaden the collection and balance its elite emphasis by gathering a wide variety of people's stories. The museum has aggressively
pursued an oral history program to interview a broad cross-section
of narrators: generally to document stories of experience, point
of view, and way of life, and specifically to enrich the museum's
mission-driven emphasis on work, workers, and the workplace.

Three projects gave us the opportunity to sharpen our focus on such stories and incorporate new perspectives into the larger collection, suggesting compelling ways to retell and rehear these stories in our galleries and programs.

First, the older level of our collections supported an interpretation of World War II as the Good War. There was plenty of material to interpret industrial success at Boeing and at Puget Sound shipyards, men in uniform, and civilian defense. What we did not have were personal accounts that we could use to interpret recruitment of African American workers to Seattle that boomed that community's population by 400%. We could not interpret the recruitment, training, and experience of women workers, the wartime Rosie the Riveter. We could not interpret internment of people of Japanese descent from Seattle. We could not interpret the effects of wartime shortages, anxiety, rationing, and discipline on families. We could not interpret Seattle as a quintessential home-front city, working and partying twenty-four hours a day. Our ongoing *Homefront* project intentionally gathered stories to redress these omissions. We were able to interview a conscientious objector, a wartime labor organizer, a newspaper editor, a number of Black shipyard and Boeing workers, housewives, a Seattle policeman, and women industrial workers. These interviews gathered stories that deeply enriched our interpretation of the wartime home front and richly nuanced our interpretation of artifacts. Displaying a B-29 model as a triumph of engineering was very different than displaying a B-29 model as the product of many hands in multiple production, the funding of war bonds, the hectic world of the home front, the reward of the cost-plus contract, the product of a work force more than 55% female and about 9% African American, the plane that delivered atomic bombs to Japan, *and* a triumph of engineering that would stand Boeing in good stead during the Cold War. These were stories that had not been publicly told; they needed to be voiced. The *Homefront* oral history interviews entered the library, and their stories transformed gallery interpretations in written labels and photograph captions. They provide us new ways to engage the public in an unspoken history. Consider, for instance, given our twenty-first-century ears, the impact of the following account of Rosie the Riveter's experience by Inez Sauer:

> One day in 1942, there was a big splash in the Seattle papers. Boeing would be interviewing for women workers, no experience necessary. I

went right to work in the tool room. My supervisor said that he'd never heard of such a thing as putting women in factories, and that it was certainly not going to work out. He said, "The happiest day of my life will be when Boeing decides they can't use women, and I can be there personally to kick them out the door!"

Second, our attempts to broaden the interpretive framework received a boost when the Washington state superintendent of public instruction developed a school-to-work initiative, designed to help middle-school and high-school kids explore a broad range of jobs and to better prepare themselves for those jobs. We had interviews in the collection with CEOs, but we had none that described the work of ordinary people. We took advantage of the opportunity to record audio and video interviews for our collection with a diverse group of workers across the whole face of information technology in 2002, manufacturing in 2003, and food industries in 2004. These videotaped interviews explored in detail what people did all day, the kinds of challenges they faced in their jobs, and what their pathway was to those jobs. The superintendent of public instruction developed curriculum from our interviews for classroom use, and the museum ended up with interviews that ranged from a CNC (Computer Numerical Control) mill operator to a winemaker, a glass artist, a chemist, a machinist, a guitar maker, a web-based marketer, a farmer, a cabinet maker, and on and on. This project was an important development for two reasons: (1) the curriculum offered new ways for these stories to be heard again and again by new audiences, and (2) we learned new aspects of Seattle's industrial history from the people who lived it. As the museum's historian, I would give a great deal to have the equivalent interview sets from the 1930s or the 1960s. We used the opportunity offered by these interviews to gather artifacts that enriched the recorded stories: the chemist's lab equipment, a guitar built by the guitar maker, software developed by the software designer. The integration of collecting artifacts with oral histories was a big step forward.

Third, Tim Milewski, director at Seattle's Annex Theater, approached the museum with a partnership idea that became the next step in the museum's efforts to broaden its collection, enrich its interpretation, and engage its audience. He wanted to follow in the rich tradition of Studs Terkel's *Working* and John Bowe's *Gig* and interview people talking about their jobs, but he planned to develop and stage a readers' theater script based on this material. *Working* was a bestselling anthology of oral history interview excerpts and had become a much-talked-about musical, but Milewski was particularly inspired by the *Laramie Project*. In the *Laramie Project*, actors from the Tectonic Theater Project conducted extensive oral history interviews to explore the little Wyoming town where Matthew Shepard had been brutally murdered. The actor/interviewers then portrayed their subjects in a scripted theater experience, which *Time Magazine* described as "a new genre, a radical redefinition of what theater is capable of." Tom wanted to create a theater experience that shared the *Laramie Project*'s immersive creative process, and he wanted to use it to explore Seattle's urban workplace, including the kinds of edgy worker interviews that Bowe's *Gig* had pioneered: white collar criminals, sex workers, drug dealers. He called his project *Verbatim*. The museum agreed to train his six actor/researchers in the skills of oral history, and we convinced him that their interviews should enter the museum's collection, so that the primary collection would outlive the single product. Little did we realize that this theater partnership would generate a powerful series of gallery experiences and programs that transformed our visitors' engagement with the oral history collection.

The *Verbatim* actors borrowed museum audio recording equipment and received museum copyright agreements, and each actor went out to interview eight or so Seattle people about their work. The museum's archival commitment to these hour-long interviews encouraged narrators to be frank and reflective; many interviews are sealed in part and some interviews are only available with the narrator's name withheld. Most of these archival controls end in 2010.

Milewski's script for *Verbatim* was drawn from these fifty interviews. The show opened at a downtown Seattle theater on May 22, 2002. Here are excerpts of a critic's review in *The Stranger*:

> "It's not who I am; it's how I make my money," says a $250–an-hour escort in the Annex Theatre's new production, *Verbatim*. It was cast in October, with six ensemble performers participating in interviewing Seattleites about their jobs. . . . They play minimum-wage slaves, card dealers, booksellers, former dot-commers, strippers, librarians, firefighters, teachers, and a silhouetted futurist. *Verbatim* crackles with wit and humanity, building up to a completely organic emotional payoff spun directly from the mouths of its interview subjects.

Verbatim opened at a downtown theater to a hip young crowd who laughed in all the right places. This readers' theater world of work in Seattle was filled with laid-off software engineers, dissatisfied baristas with master's degrees, and burned-out teachers. Most people who had service jobs in Seattle couldn't afford to live there. Homeless workers lived in their cars to make ends meet; workers from China and Mexico lived ten to a room, doing pickup work at local restaurants and landscaping companies.

We decided to bring the edgy play home to our museum and offer it to our usual program audience. We turned our events rental space into an impromptu theater-in-the-round and staged *Verbatim* at the museum—and we produced it literally verbatim, too, with clear warning in our publicity that the language and subject matter were frank and adult:

> Jeff and I work together at the Lusty Lady—that's a peep show downtown on First Avenue. And we also work together at the hospital as pathology lab assistants. At the Lusty Lady, my job is to allow the gentlemen to have a good time viewing all of my body in its nude glory. And my pathology duties are data entry on the computers to assisting on autopsies. Basically, in both jobs, I'm working with stiffs. (Michelle Sigler)

The realities of work, workers, and the workplace in people's own words were deeply unsettling and profoundly moving. *Verbatim* received a standing ovation in its two performances at our museum; clearly our audience was ready for this provocative, challenging material. *Verbatim* was subversive of Seattle's sense of itself as the "most livable city," a place of constant innovation, cutting-edge technology, and total employment. Its performance brought significant balance to our interpretive voice, the inclusion of the *Verbatim* interview transcripts in the museum's library continued the rebalancing of our collection, and it opened our eyes to the power of theater as a way to retell stories.

Verbatim presented real life as subject matter worthy of dramatic interpretation. By simply paying respectful attention to everyday stories, *Verbatim* nuanced the narrative of work in Seattle. Oral history produced first-person testimony about work that connected with its audience as insiders and participants, not as visitors or audience-members. *Verbatim* showed that people do not need or want palliative, comforting history. They applauded a museum program that convinced the intellect and connected with the emotions; they wanted theater that was resonant with their own experience of reality. In fact, judged against the standard of personal experience, through its efforts to record and retell a wide range of stories from all segments of the population, the museum earned another kind of authenticity aside from that conferred by its artifacts.

After the performance, visitors spoke about similar jobs-from-hell they had had, about being laid off, about their work being out-sourced, about frustrating bosses, and about feeling unfulfilled by their jobs. They were eager to tell those stories to one another, and they spoke with a heightened sense of performance, of the dramatic power of the spoken word. For two hours, they had listened to profes-sional actors speak the plain language of ordinary people, whose sto-ries rang so true. That public experience of private stories changed the way each person regarded the history of their own lives. What if we offered the audience the chance to become the performers? And what if we followed the pathway suggested by *Verbatim*, that we mine our own growing collection of oral history interviews to develop a readers' theater script where those stories could be retold?

To test this, we experimented with a simple readers' theater— not as elaborate or rehearsed as *Verbatim*—but just a set of direc-tor's chairs and four museum volunteers, dressed in black. Our first script explored the World War II home-front oral history col-lection, offering brief stories about war, internment, family, race, work, and daily life, edited for clarity and style and organized the-matically. Our readers simply sat spot-lit at one end of a darkened room and read their paragraphs, one after the other, from scripts on music stands. We tested the readers' theater as a free public pro-gram, publicizing it with friendly journalists and to our own e-mail list as an experiment. We packed the house. At first, the audience rustled uneasily when a Black woman read the memory of a Nisei internee—they thought we'd made a mistake. But the readers were deliberately mis-sorted to their stories, a step beyond *Verbatim*. And one could tell the readers weren't actors—they didn't speak or move like professional actors, they spoke like people off the street. And once the audience became accustomed to a Nisei man reading the reminiscence of a white Rosie the Riveter, they began to listen differently, to imagine more powerfully, to separate the experience from the experiencer, the testimony from the testifier. They real-ized that the readers were sliding into one persona after another, that at any time, a white woman could speak the experience of a white male shipfitter, a Black female welder, or a white male politi-cian. The story became independent of the storyteller: it belonged to everyone, to anyone who would retell it and imagine the experi-ence described.

At Boeing, you worked in a pretty clean atmosphere. But in some of them ships! You hang upside down, you crawl through the double bottoms. The smoke was awful from welding that galvanized steel! You might have three or four men welding down there, and only one manhole with a little sucker fan. After you got off a shift, you could tell if you had too much of that smoke—everything tasted sweet. A cigarette was sweet. Everything. And you'd wake up at 3 am, and you'd freeze and sweat, and freeze and sweat. The boss kept saying, Drink lots of milk; you'll be okay. One shop I worked at, they used to hand all the welders a quart of half and half every day, to counteract that galvanize. (Wilfred Miller)

The program evaluations were very strong, and people said aloud, "You know, what I liked most about the readers' theater was that I think I could do that myself. And it would be interesting to be somebody else and tell their story." Our audience continued to guide our readers' theater program forward, suggesting more experimental directions.

So next, we tried to remove the division between performers and audience. We appealed for a group from the readers' theater audience to join us a week later to read the script in an informal circle one afternoon. These readings were quite popular, and our list of e-mail addresses made it easy to find participants. We found that readers wanted to return again and again to read different parts; they sent e-mails saying, "I want to read on Thursday but I don't want to be Reader 1 again; Reader 3 has all the best stories." In evaluations, one reader noted, "I was fascinated to be reading perspectives that I didn't agree with. . . . I felt a special responsibility to do justice to them." Another wrote, "I felt like I was performing, but even more, I felt like the other readers were performing—I really paid attention to their every word." The readers' theaters claimed a special place for retold story.

We also developed a set of two readers' theater scripts for classroom use, with a curriculum guide suggesting activities and lessons that linked this work to the state educational standards in social studies and language arts. The first script explored the Klondike Gold Rush and was drawn from diaries, letters, and newspaper accounts. The second was adapted from the adult World War II home-front script. The recommended staging is simple, but it does transform the classroom—teachers usually arrange the desks in a circle and have kids read in turn, or they bring selected readers to the front of the class. Teachers tell us in their evaluations that their kids are very conscious that as they read their stories, they are creating a piece of theater. The dramatic form makes it easy to slide into the persona of someone else. Kids are liberated by the requirements of performance, in a sense, to speak with a different voice and to "try on" a different identity and experience, walking in someone else's shoes but without the heavy demands of a traditional script and staging. Consider the impact of the following story on a Chicano high school student who is asked to read it, speaking the words and imagining the feelings of the Japanese American student who originally told the story:

I didn't realize the enormity of the situation until the next day, when I went to school. Even some of the teachers were saying, "You people bombed Pearl Harbor," and all of a sudden I became Japanese instead of the American that I had thought I was.

We thought our parents were in jeopardy because they were not citizens. We never thought that we, American citizens, were in any danger. But we all felt paranoid; very conspicuous, because of the curfew. When we went to the internment camp, we were told we could carry only two things, and we could only take what we could carry in our two hands. We had never gone traveling before, and we didn't own any suitcases. So my folks went down and purchased some cheap luggage for us.

We were herded like cattle. It was just such a different way of being dealt with. And if internment was for our protection, why were all the guns pointed inward, at us? (Akiko Kurose)

Currently, the museum is testing a true drop-in readers' theater in the galleries, with museum visitors. On a recent Saturday, we arranged five chairs around a table, and then smilingly asked visitors if they were willing to try an experiment, to test a new idea in our gallery. If asked, we told them that we were going to ask them to read a script out loud with us. When four visitors had gathered, we sat down with them and gave each one of them a copy of the *Homefront* readers' theater script, in which the paragraphs were numbered 1, 2, 3, 4, 5, and so on throughout the script. We briefly introduced the experiment, making it clear that these experiences were gathered from recorded oral history interviews, that the stories were real. We explained that the museum staffer would read aloud all the paragraphs marked 1, and that the person on the left would read aloud all the ones marked 2, and so on around the table. Our visitors either liked the experience a lot or were embarrassed, uncomfortable, or bewildered. Some people

Photo by Kathleen Knies/Museum of History & Industry

Readers participate in the Homefront readers' theater gallery program, reading the edited oral history experiences of the four characters whose photographs are on the table.

found it difficult to read aloud, for a variety of reasons, from the type being too small to English being a second language to lack of familiarity with words like "Nisei" or "plutonium." Other people reveled in the experience, often writing, "If this is acting, I'm an actor!" or "This was very moving." Gallery visitors in 2006 were amazed by a *Homefront* experience like the following, especially as the story is a puzzle whose unfolding meaning only becomes clear at its conclusion:

> We knew we weren't welcome in most of the fancy restaurants in downtown Seattle. There weren't any signs, like in the South, but the policy was well known. I had a bitter experience during the war. I was early for a job interview, and I stopped in at a little sandwich shop and sat at the counter. It was a very warm day, and I stopped in for something cool to drink. I sat and sat, and eventually was told, We don't serve you here.
>
> I said, What do you mean—you don't serve me?
>
> And he replied, We don't serve Negroes.
>
> Now we had known to avoid the bigger restaurants, but a little place like that—well, that was new. The owner must have moved up from the South, and brought his prejudices with him. (Arline Yarbrough)

Young people slid easily into the various personae and unanimously noted their familiarity with role-playing games on their evaluations. Better educated, more affluent museum goers seemed to find the readers' theater more engaging. Older visitors in family groups often helped younger visitors with their lines or with a hard word. Some people wanted to always read the same character and balked at being a union organizer one moment and a waitress the next. But when the experience worked, it seemed miraculous. Participants' voices changed, their seated manner grew more formal, their hands became expressive, and they tried to invest their reading with gravitas, emotion, and conviction. It is dangerous to draw conclusions from our small sampling, and we continue to experiment with this way of sharing stories.

We are working to develop a script that is more contemporary, that draws on the *Verbatim* collection, and we plan to try that as a drop-in readers' theater in the gallery. Perhaps it would also be wise to try, in the gallery application, scripting only five "characters" for four visitors plus one staffer, developing a home-front workplace drama among them—a conflict on the bus, a tavern debate, or some shared experience from their five different perspectives. If we remain flexible and responsive, our ongoing experiments will bring us closer and closer to a gallery experience that is intimate and powerful, transformative and unique. In the development of this program, each step along the way has built on the previous one, and at every step, it has been museum patrons who have suggested the way ahead. It is important that we continue to be guided by the visitors we hope to engage as participants and that we continue our emphasis on personal stories drawn from oral history. In this work, we have found good ways to liberate the narratives from the archive's shelves and to put them to work with each new retelling of the stories. Part of the success is due to the range of perspectives in the oral history collection and part of it has come from the participatory nature of the retelling, which gives the reader a role in narration and a way to identify with the past.

As people read aloud the stories of others, they become eager to tell and record their own stories, and it is essential that the museum's galleries and programs provide the means. "If *these* stories are important," participants say, "then my own stories are important, too." The museum has offered drop-in oral history interviews in the gallery, conducting impromptu oral history with visitors and giving them a CD or cassette of their interview. These drop-in interviews became enormously popular, and they demonstrated that the museum valued the stories of our community. Occasionally, the museum has held a topical interview day of scheduled interviews to gather stories about hundred-year-old King Street Station or memories of the death of Reverend Martin Luther King. The *Speaking of Seattle* oral history program has continued to grow, recording interviews with mayors and activists, housewives and teachers to build our collection. The museum remains focused on its primary mission to interpret Seattle work, workers, and the workplace, but we have broadened our collection far beyond stories of heroic industrial success:

> Zaaz.com was looking like a new brand of company. We had a lot of good projects and a lot of good money coming in. Which inevitably led to, "Let's buy this building on First Avenue and completely tear down the inside, keep the façade, and remodel the interior to make it this dot-com palace." It had fur-lined booths, for chrissakes! There was this booth that looked like a submarine. It's still there, with portholes and purple and orange fur on the walls. That was our meeting room. And we would huddle in the booth for conferences with clients. It was insane. Extravagant. No other way you can describe it.
>
> We threw a party there. The open house was a big success. We hired a couple of security guards downstairs to not let the riffraff in. And everybody coming in envied us for working in such a great place. And everybody was just oohing and aahing about it. A few months later, the layoffs began. (Andy Rusu)

A history museum needs to build community among its visitors, to satisfy basic curiosity about the past and to offer a place for learning and discussion about the present and the future. But the museum should also disorient its visitors somewhat. One way to accomplish this is to offer our visitors a point of departure that begins on familiar ground and slowly leads to a pathway toward more adventuresome, perhaps dangerous, stories that differ from their own. The most effective learning begins where we are and moves outward from there. An oral history readers' theater offers a magical chance to step into someone else's shoes and begin to walk outward from oneself. That's the value of the retellings.

The museum's collaboration with the state superintendent of public instruction and a young director from a downtown theater company have had many positive outcomes. The collection of interviews about contemporary work and workers grew by more than a hundred interviews in less than three years. This critical mass encouraged other work-focused interviewing projects—a set with labor and community organizers, a set with environmental activists, and so on. These resources have found their way into exhibitions, programs, and on-line features, but the museum's gallery experiments with participatory readers' theaters have been most provocative and intriguing. During the last five years, our museum's galleries and programs have become infused by the power of storytelling.

Public institutions, such as museums, play a vital role in providing a space to retell and rehear oral accounts. Each recorded oral history in the museum's collection is a unique performance by the narrator as he or she crafted experiences into a story to be shared with others, into the distant future. In one use, the evidence of oral history interviews in the museum's collection has helped to balance the collection and dissented from the comfortable generalizations of a therapeutic historical narrative. Oral history literally spoke truth to power. In a second use, actors and our visitors have been able to use edited oral history scripts to understand and identify with the original speakers, as they internalized the original experiences and externalized them in their own portrayals. As oral historians, we provide the means for members of our community to tell such stories to the present and future about their perceptions of the past. Their words don't stand alone nor do they stand still: they are contexted and mediated by gender, class, and ethnicity; by time and place; and by personality, memory, and style of personal expression.

A story's telling and retelling generates a set of translations into various languages of performance. Participatory readers' theater is one possible performance mode among many based on the museum's collection of oral history interviews. Deliberately shorn of contextual associations, these scripts *insist* on words standing alone and call upon readers and listeners to provide their own context and understanding, to imagine themselves in the experiences they are reading aloud. As museum visitors mediate the experiences of Seattle residents, living and dead, through their own experience, speaking the words of others with their own voices, they engage with the past in ways that no static exhibit can offer. Their role play in a virtual reality is enabled by the power of their script and the recorded memories on which the script was based. Starting with their own experience, visitors read their way across the bridge of story to new places, new roles to play, and new realities to understand.

Performance/Participation

A Conversation with Lorraine McConaghy and
Karen R. Utz

Lorraine McConaghy and Karen Utz describe how
they create settings for retelling oral history. In contrast to the Kirin Narayan-Barre Toelken discussion,
which centered on participation by cultural members in their own traditions, these authors focus on
creating contexts for people unfamiliar with traditions to experience the stories. Their goal is to present aspects of the historical narrative in the words of
the original narrators and thereby create a greater
awareness of the fuller dimensions of local history.

SCHNEIDER: Karen, I know from reading about your work that you,
like Lorraine, have used oral history to retell the story of the people
who worked in the Birmingham blast furnaces. Do you see some
parallels in the way both of you use stories to relate the experiences
of people whose narratives have not been represented in historic
interpretation?

UTZ: You know, like Lorraine said in her paper, a history museum
needs to build community among its visitors. This particular site,
Sloss Furnaces, depended for decades on cheap Black labor. African
Americans were paid a lot better than they used to be as sharecrop-
pers but they still weren't paid all that well. The work was brutal,
and they were never allowed to have management positions until

---

Karen R. Utz is curator at Sloss Furnaces National Historic Landmark, where
she conducts various research and writing projects and interprets the history of industrialization and technology in the American South. She is also
adjunct history instructor at the University of Alabama at Birmingham. Her
work at Sloss highlights the social and economic conditions of life at the
furnaces in the Birmingham Industrial District. Like McConaghy, her primary focus is presentation of history to the public. An example of this is
her essay, "Goin' North: The African-American Women of Sloss Quarters"
in *Work, Family, Faith: Southern Women in the Twentieth-Century South*, edited by
Melissa Walker and Rebecca Sharpless (2006) Recently, she edited *Man Food:
Recipes from the Iron Trade, Sloss Furnaces National Historic Landmark* (2007).

the 1960s. So, with that in mind, we now offer a variety of programs that give back to the African American community by giving voice to their experiences. Just as Lorraine has used oral history to record a broader and more representative history of Seattle, we are trying to tell a more inclusive story about the experiences of the actual workers who made pig iron and their wives and children who lived in company housing, shopped at the commissary, and were treated at the infirmary. Before I began work here, women had never been interviewed and I knew women had lived here; there were forty-eight company houses. So when I interviewed the women, I knew something had to be done with their stories. I took the traditional route of submitting an essay for the book *Work, Faith, and Family*, and that has been a valuable way to get the women's stories retold. We have relied on our school outreach programs and the character of Little Red, an African American man from Green County, Alabama, who worked at Sloss Furnace in the 1920s. One of our staff members, Ron Bates, visits classrooms and tells stories about what it was like to work at a blast furnace. Working from a script based on oral history, he impersonates Little Red. The teacher and students ask Little Red questions and he tells them about his work experiences. Little Red talks about the harshness and the danger in the type of work that was done breaking up the pig iron and tapping the furnace. He emphasizes how the workers contributed to the industry and the community that grew up in the company housing, known as the Quarters. Little Red was a great first baseman for the Sloss's Black baseball team, the Raggedy Roaches. Clarence Dean, a fellow who worked at Sloss for years and lived in the Quarters for over twenty years, once said that "Sloss had one of the best [Black] ball teams you wanted to see."

So what we are trying to show is that the average worker did work hard, grueling jobs and they contributed a great deal, such as developing some of the new techniques for breaking up pig iron. And most importantly, men like Little Red took a great deal of pride in their work and even though there was discrimination in who could hold which jobs, the big joke was once you got in the furnace area and you came out covered in soot and ash, no one knew who was Black or White anyway. Our job is to record, preserve, and find ways to retell those stories.

MCCONAGHY: To me when the museum records an oral history, we are recording stories that have been told within a family and now we are sort of freezing them in time, documenting them for the collection indefinitely. It's not as if we create those stories by documenting them. On the contrary, we document something living and then it ends up on the shelf. And what has been distressing to me was that this is the most vivid, extraordinarily engaging kind of reminiscence, points of view about the past that personalize these very large striding themes that are integral parts of the social history. It seems to me our responsibility is to get these recordings back out there where they had been before we put them in a jar on the shelf. That's why I'm excited about the work we are doing with the public readings. The readings get the stories back out.

UTZ: That's a very good point and you did it in such a creative way and you did it in a community way. These stories are inherently interesting and people are eager to learn about and identify with the people and events described. Our approach has been less participatory and more directed at interpreting the history to an audience. In our reenactments, the visitors meet the characters and interact with them but they are not asked to directly take on the persona of the character. For instance, the city of Birmingham had something they called Discover Birmingham, where the public could go to different museums around town. Well, the last stop at eight o'clock at night was an historical ghost tour of Sloss Furnace. It was dark and we lit the place up with candles and we had various characters at different stations: we had Little Red down in the tunnel reenacting the activities of that place, and I was Sarah Jowers, the wife of Theo Jowers, a White worker who lost his life when he fell into the top of the furnace while changing the charging bell, so the story goes. It's called a bell because of its bell-shape design, but it is a devise located at the top of the furnace that keeps the gasses from escaping. Theo must have slipped while working on it. (To understand the full impact of this death, you have to recognize that many of the visitors recognized how dangerous work was at the furnace and the image of a man falling into the furnace is a terrible thought, but not one hard for our visitors to imagine.) So, they had these tours of thirty-five in a group that would come down in the tunnel, and the character portraying the worker would talk about what he went through. Then they would go through the blowing engine building, the oldest building on site, and the last stop was me. As Sarah Jowers, I told the story about what happened to my husband. In retelling this story, I was building on several sources. The Jowers did settle here, and he did fall into the top of a furnace. The account was reported in the book *The Ghost in Sloss Furnaces* by Kathryn Tucker Windham [1978], and, the story goes, over the years, as each blast furnace shut down, workers swore they saw his image at their site. I've interviewed various sound-minded workers and that's what they say. They are very serious about this. Sloss was the last furnace left in Birmingham. The story goes that Theo's ghost came here in the fifties, and to this day, as you walk around here, you supposedly can see his image. So when I played the role of Sarah, it was a good way for me to personalize the story of Birmingham as a center of iron production. This was heavy on interpretation and it took place in the furnace, so the setting was authentic.

SCHNEIDER: So, in your portrayal of Sarah Jowers and in Little Red's reenactment you are drawing on the written and oral sources, but what else do you draw upon to bring the stories to life. Does Little Red dress the part?

UTZ: Absolutely. I don't think a lot of these kids in the schools see people in overalls and leathers. Leathers are pieces of leather you strap around your calves in order not to get burned when you tap the furnace. I think he occasionally takes the pair of wooden shoes once used by the workers. If you are going to work around pig iron you've got to have these wooden-soled shoes. And I think because he dresses in this manner, it just gives it more credibility and gets the kids to sit up and take notice a bit. The clothing makes all the difference. I also think the dialect helps a great deal. Little Red speaks in a regional dialect, the area he is from, and he says: "I always get questions when I leave. 'Do you really talk like that?'" Then he explains that his grandparents who came from Green County actually did talk that way.

SCHNEIDER: Lorraine, Karen is using a lot of props and background to retell her stories, but yours thrive on the power of the narrative.

McCONAGHY: Well, I think the thing that was most fun for me was that our audience, the visitors to our galleries, pushed our project further and further along by telling us, "If that's a performance, then I'm a performer," or "If that's history, I've lived history"; they wanted to participate in reader's theatre. They told us that. So it was step by step. As I point out in the paper, it is an imperfect experience at times because English is a second language for some of our visitors and some are embarrassed about how well they read. But when it works, it works extremely well, and people say it was really neat to be in someone else's shoes.

SCHNEIDER: That's an interesting point because we think oral history is built on a relationship between the narrator who tells their story and an audience. In the case of one-on-one interviewing, there is a give and take between the narrator and the interviewer, with the interviewer seeking clarification or elaboration and in some cases guiding the interview. In the case of a narrator who is addressing an audience, he or she may be building on a speaker who spoke before or may have in his mind the need to speak in reference to and at a particular occasion. But what you are describing, Lorraine, builds solely on the strength of the story as revealed in a written transcript, no background research by the speaker, no props to convey an identity, no context. Your readers are coming at this totally cold. Nowhere are they told how to read the script.

McCONAGHY: Yes, and I don't want to suggest that I have no respect for the oral history interview as a document. I do. We work very hard to videotape all our interviews because we have so much respect for how people express themselves. In a sense this is an *application*, one product of dozens that one might imagine from the basic oral history document. The video remains there as the ultimate reference. It's just that this is an edited use of these oral history experiences. They are true statements about the experiences of individuals, experiences that we can imagine but that are different from our own. When we put the stories in the mouths of people who didn't experience the events described, we create an opportunity for them to take on someone else's point of view. That is what is most exciting to me. You know, when a Japanese American girl reads the memories of an African American man, this is where performance and participation blur and where that girl may begin to imagine and take on, in a small way, the reality of the African American man's experience. These stories can have a vivid life in someone else's mouth! But without good oral history, this program goes nowhere; oral history is the grist for the mill.

SCHNEIDER: While both of you are creating public spaces for the retelling of stories, the interesting thing to me is that the stories you are retelling are ones that have not been afforded the recognition nor given the public space before. Lorraine, you are correct that good oral history is the foundation of the work, but I would also add that both of you have recognized through the oral history that there is a bigger story than has been told before, and you have been effective in not only bringing that to light but also giving visitors a chance to experience the story. Both approaches, the participatory approach that you use, Lorraine, and the interpretative approach you use, Karen, offer equally effective but different types of experience for the visitor or classroom student.

Afterword

William Schneider

Yogi Berra, baseball star and colorful ex-manager of the New York Yankees and New York Mets, is credited with saying, "It ain't over till it's over." It is as true for stories as it is for baseball and life in general. Our understanding of a story is never complete, because each time we hear the story told it may speak to us in a different way. Telling and hearing stories, one to another, is a creative act. The range of possibilities is endless, expanding each time the story is told and discussed. As Finnegan (1998) reminds us, the oral narrative, unlike the written account, is retold a new each time and within a new context. It ain't over till people stop telling it . . . but then is it really over? What happens when someone dusts off the recording on the shelf and tries to reconstruct meaning, tries to retell the story?

For both the living traditions where we can engage the teller to discuss meaning and the recordings of those who have passed on, the approach and questions are similar. We want to know how the group of people use(d) the story to convey meaning. We recognize that all stories are told within a context and tradition bearers must understand their audiences as well as their stories, and they must tailor their retellings to communicate effectively to their cultural group. In some cases, there are very strict protocols on how stories can be told, such as in Northwest Coast Indian clan stories, or the Navajo stories about places described by Klara Kelley in this volume, where there are very strict rules on who can tell the story and how it can be used. In other cases, stories are open to a wider range of interpretation and use, as in the story of "The Giant Footprints" described by Holly Cusack-McVeigh in her paper. When we know some of the rules for how stories can be used, it helps us reconstruct some of the parameters of expression and intended meaning. Individuals who grow up in the tradition and know the storytellers are guides to our understanding of how narrative is used.

Consider, for instance, the reception Kirin Narayan received when she brought back the recording of the women's wedding song and how her friends responded by adding verses to a familiar theme, a point elaborated on by Barre Toelken in his discussion of the dynamics operating in song recall.

In this series of essays, we have emphasized that our most fundamental guide is our experience listening to the story over multiple tellings and by different tellers, living with the story, the people who tell it, and the records they leave behind. This means finding out how people used the story in the past, documenting how they use it today, and recognizing how we incorporate and use the story in our own life as well. The author's relationship with the storyteller and the experiences they share are critical to our understanding of how the story told on a particular occasion connects to the cultural tradition. For instance, Holly Cusack-McVeigh's essay on Yup'ik oral tradition is based on her personal experiences with Yup'ik friends who told her the story of the Giant Footprints because they thought she needed to learn the lessons it could teach. Her personal experiences with her friends created the context and need for the telling and the lesson. Barbara Babcock and Joanne Mulcahy echo the connection between the intimacy of a telling and the tradition from which it springs. They lament how often the relationship between storytellers and writers and the basis of their sharing goes unexplored in publications. Similarly, in his discussion of Kirin Narayan's work with Indian women's marriage songs, Barre Toelken finds a strong analogy between the intimacy of women sharing a traditional wedding song and the men in his family sharing a seafaring ballad from their ancestor's whaling days. In each case the personal relationships, experiences shared, and recollections of how the story or song has been told in the past add layers of meaning to the present recollection and retelling.

Elsewhere I have drawn a distinction between oral tradition and oral history (1995:189–202, 2002: 53–66). I claimed that oral tradition consists of the stories that a group of people know, that they consider important enough to retell, and that they actually do retell and pass on to others. I still think this is true but now I also recognize, even for stories no longer told by a group, that if the record of past tellings is complete enough we should be able to reconstruct how, why, and when a story was told. And we may be able to speculate with a fair degree of assurance the intended meaning understood by those who shared in the tradition. If oral tradition is bound to a group that in some ways shares common understandings, then what is oral history? Oral history is the act of recording and creating a record of the narrative exchange. Of course, stories need not be bound to a particular tradition. We can and do learn and use stories outside of our particular traditions. This is the point of Lorraine McConaghy's and Karen Utz's work. But in these cases, our understanding is limited by our lack of experience with how the story has been used and the tradition in which the story derives its meaning. For instance, I am richer because of Joanne Mulcahy's description of Eva Castellanoz and how she uses the metaphor of "healing the root." but how much more I could understand if I knew Eva, was steeped in Mexican American culture, and could sense the response of the young people in the audience as she tells them that life is like a tree: if the roots aren't healthy, the tree won't survive. Part of our challenge then in oral history is to preserve as much of the social and cultural setting along with the words recorded on the machine. We need those clues to explain how the story is used over time and the reasons for differences in emphasis and content. As the essays in this volume demonstrate, stories can be illusive. They evolve over time as the storyteller seeks ways to add perspective to the present with knowledge from the past. In Sherna Gluck's essay on the story of the woman's role in the first Palestinian *intifada*, the story becomes layered with new interpretation as time and circumstances call for a particular emphasis. Sometimes it is a matter of opportunity to tell one's story. For instance, in Aron Crowell and Estelle Oozevaseuk's discussion of the St. Lawrence Island famine, the clan story emerges at the Smithsonian and provides a counter-narrative to the published accounts. James Clifford, commenting on the paper, sees this emergence as a reflection of the need all people have to place their versions of history in the record, versions that reflect their interpretations, perspectives, and values. The setting provided an opening for the story to be told.

These dynamics also operate at the personal level with stories that become important to us individually but aren't part of the cultural tradition, the stories that we choose to tell based on our own experience, witness to a devastating flood, an experience at war, or a wilderness trek. We shape and retell these stories because we think they are important. What guidelines do we have to understand what they mean? Our beacon here, as with oral tradition, is the retelling, the record of their tellings, and our experiences with the narrator and the historical record. Our focus is both back in time to the era when the event took place, so we understand the conditions at that time, and to the present when the story is being told so we can appreciate why it is being retold. As with oral tradition, the more we listen to how the story is told and understood by others the more we appreciate its range of meaning and how it is used. This is particularly true of "signature stories." These are personal stories that reflect a life-shaping experience that become, for the teller, a lesson or way to look at the current situations that he or she faces. As the term suggests, signature stories become identified with the individuals who tell them and the way they use them. For my parents' generation, the Great Depression became a signature story to remind their children of hard times and the importance of saving.

I grew up hearing Depression stories at the Sunday dinner table. They conveyed lessons my elders had learned through personal experience and now felt compelled to pass on. In this case, the meaning of the stories is closely tied to their experiences and may have little meaning for my daughter and other youth, two generations removed from the event. Howard Luke, an Athabascan Indian who lives near me in Fairbanks, grew up during the Depression. His Depression story is tied to the theme of self-sufficiency. He says, when the tough times come, "my dollar will be worth more than yours." This is his way of emphasizing how important it is to learn to live on the land and have the skills to survive without much money. In both stories, (the ones I grew up with and the one I have heard several times from Howard), my understanding comes from knowing the individuals very well and hearing their story told many times. In fact, the individuals and how I know them is so much a part of my understanding of what they mean that it is hard for me to sort out the words from the person. And that is the nature of this work; we are challenged to get beyond words to meaning, our personal understanding of the story and the storyteller. Familiarity between teller and listener breeds both understanding and confidence and allows us to see how the story is used over time. As we saw, Sherna Gluck's understanding of how her interviewees described the women's role in the Palestinian *Intifada* evolved as they responded to the politics of the time, refusing to be reduced to a single description for all time. And in her work with the woman representing the garment worker's union, she found that a fuller story was forthcoming only after a second visit, when the person better understood and trusted her intent.

As oral historians, we are called upon to reconstruct the social and cultural meanings of each story, not seeking boundaries and reconciliation of positions but instead seeing the opportunities where tellers engaged their audience with explanation, personal perspective, and cultural insight. But as Aron Crowell and Estelle Oozevaseuk caution us in their article, we need to look beyond the fit of the evidence to the cultural and personal interpretations and the settings where the story re-emerges. How easy and misguided it would have been to place one account against the other in an attempt to reconcile discrepancies. As oral historians we are compelled to explore the convergences and the divergences and preserve the various articulations of the story for this and future generations (Kline 1996:9–39). We owe it to future generations of oral historians who will be called upon to retell the story. By creating opportunities for the story to be retold, we preserve a fuller oral history record. And as Lorraine McConaghy and Karen Utz point out, oral historians have a responsibility to engage the public with stories of those who came before, particularly those whose historical voice has not been heard. They argue that retelling is a way of preserving the story, a way to create a contact between a person whose story sits on the shelf and a museum visitor who is invited to be that character and share their experience for a little while. Their work is testimony to how reading narratives aloud or experiencing a reenactment can trigger a reader or listener's imagination and discovery of meaning even when they are new to a subject.

In the end, it is our contact with the teller (real in the case of those we interview and imagined in the case of those whose recordings we hear or whose transcripts we are called to read) that allows us to see ourselves in the experience described, to live with the story, and perhaps, at the right moment in our own lives when we find meaning in the experience recalled, when the analogy with the present is compelling, when there is a point to be made, a lesson to be learned, we will choose to retell the story. The essays in this volume represent more than a record of events; like all good stories, they are lessons to live by, reminders of how to treat animals, the land, each other. That is why they are important and will continue to be retold. It ain't really ever over, nor should it be!

References

Finnegan, Ruth. 1998. *Oral Literature in Africa*. Oxford: Oxford University Press.

Kline, Carrie. 1996. "Giving it Back: Creating Conversations to Interpret Community Oral History." *Oral History Review*. Vol. 19, 9–39.

Laughlin, William S. 1980. *Aleuts: Survivors of the Bering Land Bridge.* New York: Holt, Rinehart & Winston.

Schneider, William. 1995. "Lessons from Alaska Natives about Oral Traditions and Recordings." In *When our Words Return: Writing, Hearing, and Remembering Oral Traditions of Alaska and the Yukon,* Phyllis Morrow and William Schneider, eds., 185–204. Logan: Utah State University Press.

Schneider 2002. *...So They Understand: Cultural Issues in Oral History.* Logan: Utah State University Press.

Index

Illustrated matter is indicated by italics.
Numbers in parentheses following note numbers
indicate text pages that those notes annotate.

A

abus, rule of, 130, 131
African Americans, oral histories of, 143, 151, 155–56
Agnaga (woman of Uwaliit clan), 57
Akenfield, 4
Alaska Native Claims Settlement Act, 71
alcohol use by Yup'ik Eskimo: alcohol traded for meat, 48; Euro-American perspectives on, 43, 44, 45, 46–47; indigenous perspectives on, 40, 41, 50; origin of, 42
Ale'qat (Asiatic Eskimo), 49, 70
al-Labadi, Fadwa. *See* Labadi, Fadwa al-
Allen, Barbara, 6–7, 11
alternative (non-official) histories: museum presentation of, 140; native, 13, 36–37, 49, 50–59, 68–73, 163; political climate influence on, 134, 135, 136
Amalgamated Clothing Workers of America (ACWA), 137
American Folklore Society, 23
American Oral History Association, 3, 6, 7, 10, 120
American West, stories on, 6–7
Amoskeag, 4
ancient site role in behavioral instruction, 14, 18, 28, 35
ancient texts, 8, 9
animals, Yup'ik Eskimo beliefs concerning: hunting, 29n1 (20), 57, 59; mistreatment, consequences of, 13, 36, 51, 55–56; respect, emphasis on, 56–57, 58, 59, 73
Aningayou, James, 55–56
anthropological history, 5
anthropology, 2–3, 5
Apache storytelling, 29n10 (28)
Apassingok, Anders, 59, 70

Arab-Israeli War, 1948–1949, 122
Arab Women's Congress, First, Jerusalem, 1927, 122
Arafat, Yasir (Abu Amar), 130
archaeological excavations, 39–40, 61n5 (44)
Askinuk (Yup'ik Eskimo village), 19, 20, 26–27
Ataayaghaq, Jimmy, 48
Athabascan Indian stories, 164
"author" (oral history term), 6

B

Babcock, Barbara, 12, 117–18, 119, 162
Balfour Declaration, 122
bande (term), 89–90
Barghouti, Siham, 124, 125
bark as metaphor, 12, 100, 105, 106, 112
Basic Law (temporary Palestinian constitution), 131
Basso, Keith, 29n10 (28)
Bates, Ron, 156
behavior: ancient site role in teaching, 14, 18, 28, 35; Eskimo beliefs concerning proper, 11, 20–21, 22, 28
Bengali songs, 85
Berra, Yogi, 161
Bhagavad Gita (Hindu sacred text), 75
Birmingham industrial history, 14, 155–56, 157–58
birth songs, Indian (Asian), 76
Black Heritage Society of Washington State, *140*
Black railcar porters, stories of, 6
black tongue (disease), 46
Boeing workers in World War II, 143, 148
Bogoras, Waldemar, 49, 70
Bowe, John, 144

G

Gambell (Yup'ik Eskimo village, St. Lawrence Island). *See* Sivuqaq (Gambell) (Yup'ik Eskimo village, St. Lawrence Island)

gang members, stories about, 100, 111

garment workers, interviews with, 14, 164

Gaurja (Parvati) (Hindu Goddess), 75, 87

Gaza, Israeli invasion of, 122

gender: India, ideologies in, 78; issues in fieldwork, 12; Yup'ik Eskimo beliefs concerning, 18, 20–21, 22–23, 28

genealogical accounts, role in oral history, 5

genocide, public recognition of, oral history role in, 4

George Magoon and the Down East Game War (Ives), 6

George Magoon (culture hero), 6

Ghost in Sloss Furnaces, The (Windham), 158

giant ants, 33, 34

"Giant Footprints, The" ("giant footsteps") (Yup'ik Eskimo story): behavioral lessons learned through, 11, 35, 162; culture and beliefs revealed through, 18; interpretation and meaning of, 161; other stories linked to, 27, 28; personal experience connected to, 23–24; retelling of, 33; site linked to, 20–21, 31; versions, 20–21, 22–23, 25–26

gift offerings to land, Yup'ik Eskimo practice of, 24–25, 27, 28

Gig (Bowe), 144

Gluck, Sherna, 13, 14, 120, 134–35, 136–37, 163, 164

Great Depression stories, 164

H

Hasso, Frances, 121

healing: faith connection to, 106, 107, 108, 111; metaphor connection to, 12, 14, 107, 163

Henry, Douglas, 70

Here's to You, Jesusa! (Poniatowski), 119

heritage as historical voice, 69

heroes, museum presentation of, 141, 152

Hilterman, Joost, 121, 128

historical anthropology, 5

historical reconstruction, 5

historical voice, 69, 71

historic context of stories, 8–9, 10

historic events, story role in explaining, 13, 36–37, 38–39, 40–41, 68–69

historic reenactments, oral history use in, 14, 156, 157–59, 165

history: as oral history discipline, 2–3; identity, relationship to, 59, 69–70; making of, story role in, 68, 72; museum presentation of, 146–47, 152–53; participation in, 98; perceptions of past, differing in field of, 5

Holocaust, interviews on, 4

Home Front oral history project, 143–44, 149–51, *150*

homeless workers, oral histories of, 146

Hooper, Calvin L., 39, 44, 45, 46, 47

Hooper Bay (Yup'ik Eskimo village), 18–19, 20, 21–23, 27, 29, 34

hunting: laws, attitudes concerning, stories revealing, 6; by Yup'ik Eskimo, challenges facing, 43, 44, 48, 50; Yup'ik Eskimo beliefs concerning, 13, 21, 28, 29n1 (20), 55, 57, 58, 59

I

Icelandic community, life stories in, 23

identity: history, relationship to, 59, 69–70; as process, 71; trees as symbols of, 100

ILGWU (union), 137

immigrant workers, oral histories of, 146

incest, Palestinian discourse on, 129

Indian (Asian) songs, 12, 76. *See also* wedding songs, Indian (Asian)

India-Pakistan Partition, 1947, 91

indigenous groups, migrant workers from, 104

indigenous Mexican persons in Oregon, 114n6 (104)

indigenous traditions, Mexican art influenced by, 100

industrial histories, local, 14, 143–44, 155–56, 157–58

industrial progress, museum presentation of, 141

In Place (Allen), 6–7

institutional religion, E. Castellanoz on, 112

interpretation of stories, 8–9, 10
interviews: access and utilization of,
138–40, *140,* 142–44, 153–54,
156–57, 165 (*see also* reenactments,
oral history use in; theater scripts:
oral history as basis for); conducting, informal of, 138–40; history
research, role in, 3, 4; redoing, pros
and cons of, 120–21
intifada. *See* Palestinian *intifada,* first;
Palestinian *intifada,* second
Israel, declaration of independence
by, 122
Italy, modern history of, 11
Ives, Edward "Sandy," 6, 11

J

Jabalya refugee camp, auto accident
in, 122
Janmashtami festival, 75
Japanese Americans: first generation
of, 4; internment of, 141–42, 143,
147, 149
Jowers, Sarah, 157–58
Jowers, Theo, 157–58

K

Kaa_x'achgóok (Yukon legendary
figure), 7
Kamal, Zahera, 124
Kaneshiro, Oovi (Vera), 51, 70
Kangra, Northwest India, 74–75, 76,
85, 90
Kangra folksongs, 76, 97
Kelley, Klara, 11, 31–34, 161
King, Martin Luther, 152
kinship ideologies in India, 78
Klondike Gold Rush, 148
Krishna (Hindu deity): as prankster,
84, 92; disguised as woman, 79–82,
85, 86–87, 89, 90; grooms compared
to, 78; mythology of, 91; stories in
songs, 75–77; woman, beautiful,
encounter with, 12, 83, 88
Kukelek (Yup'ik Eskimo village, St.
Lawrence Island): American-
European contact with, 42;
archaeological excavations at,
39–40; clothing of, 38; famine and
epidemic impact on, 44, 47, 48, 49;
map of, *43*; narratives from, 50–55,
59, 70; prefamine description of, 45;
residents of, 41

L

Labadi, Fadwa al-, 121, 124–25
labor activists, interviewing of, 136–37,
143, 164
labor history, museum policies concerning, 141
land, relationship to, Yup'ik Eskimo
beliefs concerning, 24–25, 27, 28,
29
Laramie Project (film), 145
Latin America, political movements
in, 129
Latino youth, perceptions of, 111
legends, role in oral history, 5
lessons conveyed through stories, 165
life history method, 5–6
life stories. *See* oral history interviews;
personal experience
Little Red (African American man),
156, 157, 158
lived experience, songs as part of, 95,
96, 98
Luke, Howard, 164

M

Magmyut (Magmiuts) (Yup'ik Eskimo
people), 18, 19
married life, songs about, 76
McConaghy, Lorraine, 14, 138, 155,
156–57, 158–60, 163, 165
McVeigh, Holly Cusack. *See* Cusack-
McVeigh, Holly
meaning in stories: assigning, pitfalls
of, 10; creating and conveying, 2,
59, 161; discovering, 165; events,
explanation for, 13; new, evolution
of, 68–69, 70; range of, 8, 9; recon-
structing, 164–65; retelling role in
creating, 59; traditional, 162–63;
uncovering, 113, 164
memory: official narrative impact on,
136; place as anchor to, 31–32, 35;
present relationship to, 14, 15
menstrual practices of Yup'ik Eskimo,
18, 20–21, 22–23
menstruation, first as story motif, 29n3
(21)
metaphor: cultural differences,
transcending through, 117; use in
stories, 12, 99–100, 105, 106, 107,
112, 113. *See also* Castallenoz, Eva:
metaphor use by

connection to, 112; of foundation,
105; in healing, 111, 163
Rosie the Riveter, 143–44, 147
Rosse, Irving C., 45, 46
Rozner, Sarah, 136–137
Rukmani, Princess (Krishna's wife), 75,
77, 79–80

S

sacred zones of Navajo, 33
Sangeeta Devi, 86, 87, 90
Sansar Chand, King of Kangra
(1775–1823), 75
Santino, Jack, 6
Santora, Mamie, 137
Sauer, Inez, 143–44
saving, importance of, 164
Schneider, William, 1, 22, 40, 92
schools, readers' theaters in, 148–49
school-to-work initiative, 144
seal hunts, 20, *20*, 23, 28, 43, 45
Seattle: economic and working conditions in, 145–47; history of, 14;
industrial history of, 143–44; in
World War II, 143–44
Seattle's Museum of History & Industry,
138–39, *140*, 140–44
segregation, oral history treatment of,
151
self-sufficiency, importance of, 164
separation from God, allegories of, 84
sexual abuse, Palestinian discourse on,
129
sexual impropriety as song theme, 84
shaman's grave, Hooper Bay, 34
Shangin, Barbara, 71
Sharma, Meenakshi, 76, 85
Sharon, Ariel, 131n1 (121)
Shepard, Matthew, murder of, 145
Shiva (Hindu God), 75, 78, 87
Sidney, Angela, 7
signature stories, 164
Silko, Leslie, 117–18
Silook, Paul, 47–48, 59
Silook, Roger, 55, 72–73
Silook, Susie, 72–73
Sir! No Sir! (film), 136
sister, unknown as song theme, 81–82,
88
Sivuqaq (Gambell) (Yup'ik Eskimo
village, St. Lawrence Island): food
shortage at, 48; graves near, 44;
migration to, 41, 47; persons from,

51; population and size of, 43, 45;
renaming of, 42; residents, description of, 46
Sloss Furnaces, 155–56, 157–58
social well-being, ancient sites as
barometers of, 31, 34
songs: learning, 32; modern challenges to learning, 90; past recalled
through, 90–91, 92; recreating, 14;
role in storytelling, 12–13, 74–75;
role of, 95; variations of, 78, 85–86,
97
soul's separation from God, allegories
of, 84
Speaking of Seattle oral history project,
139, *140*, 152
spirit world, Yup'ik Eskimo beliefs
concerning, 26–27, 28
St. Lawrence Island, description and
demographics of, 41–43, *43*
St. Lawrence Island famine and epidemic, 1878–1880: environmental
and economic factors, 42; native
explanation for, 13, 36–37, 49,
50–59, 68–73, 163; official explanation for, 36–37, 43–47, 50; sources
on, 38–39, 47–50
Storytellers, Saints, and Scoundrels
(Narayan), 10
Suman (groom's mother's half-sister at
wedding): family of, 88, 91; Krishna
songs sung by, 84, 85, 86, 87;
Krishna stories told by, 83, 90, 92;
"Naglila" ("snake play") song sung
by, 79; visit with, 89
sunrise as miracle, 108
Swameji (holy man), 10
Swedenburg, Ted, 13–14, 128, 134,
135–36, 137

T

tagged potentials, 8, 9
tape recording: limitations of, 9–10;
role in history preservation, 3; written record, similarities to, 9
Tayi (Aunty) (old Indian woman), 91
Terkel, Studs, 144–45
theater scripts, oral history as basis
for, 139–40, 144–52, *150*, 153–54,
158–59
therapeutic historical perspective, 153
thickness of earth, 21, 28
Toelken, Barre, 12, 95–97, 155, 162

traditions: identification with, 95; song
role in preserving, 95; story role in
preserving, 35
transformation of stories, 2
tree as metaphor: components of, 100,
105, 106, 112, 163; in healing, 103–4;
of spiritual power, 109; Tree of Life
(cultural symbol), 12, 99, 100

U

ubuntu (Xhosa word), 8
understanding of past, evolution of,
7–8
understanding of stories, 10
Ungaziq (Old Chaplino, Indian Point)
(Yup'ik Eskimo village, St. Lawrence
Island), 41
Union of Palestinian Women's
Committees (UPWC), 126, *127,* 129
UNITE (union), 137
Upadhyay, Sarla, 79, 84
Urmilaji (Urmila Devi Sood), 77,
85–86, 87–88, 90
U.S. Oral History Association, 3, 6, 7,
10, 120
utilization of stories, 161–62, 163
Utz, Karen, 14, 155–56, 157–58, 160,
163, 165
Uwetelen (Estelle Ooozevaseuk's
grandfather), 58–59

V

"verbal arts" (term), 5
Verbatim (film), 145–47, 151
Vietnam and Other American Myths
(Franklin), 136
Vietnam veterans, treatment of, 14
Vietnam War, public opinion regard-
ing, 136
Vishnu (Hindu God), 75
Volcano Mountains, story of, 26, 27, 28
Voluntary Work Committee (VWC),
124, 125

W

walrus: depletion of, 42, 43; hunting of,
41, 43, 44, 46, 47, 55; mistreatment
of, 13, 36, 40, 51, 55–56, 57
wedding songs, Indian (Asian), 12, 13,
14, 74, 76, 77–78, 79–84, 162
West Bank, Israeli invasion and occupation of, 121–22

Western contact with St. Lawrence
Island, 42
whaling songs, 13, 95–96, 162
wife battering, Palestinian discourse on,
129, 134
Windham, Kathryn Tucker, 158
winter, storytelling restricted to, 31, 33
women labor activists, interviewing of,
136–37, 164
women's economic cooperatives, 123
women's history, museum policies
concerning, 141, 156
women's movement, Palestinian:
activists, *125;* development and
evolution of, 13, 120, 129, 130–31,
135–36; feminist consciousness,
representations of, 126–30; genera-
tional differences in, 126; leaders,
training of, 122–23; men *versus,* 124,
125; origin stories of, 121, 123–26
women's organizations, Palestinian,
122, 124, 135
women's songs: Chandravali's song,
77–84; Krishna stories in, 75–77;
occasions for, 89; past, continuity
through, 13, 91; research on, 74,
162
women's stories, 118–19
women workers in World War II,
143–44
Work, Faith, and Family, 156
workers, oral histories of, 4, 145–47,
153, 155–56
Working (Terkel), 144–45
Working Women's Committee
(Palestine), 123–26
World War II: as interview subject, 4,
143–44; interpretation of, 143–44;
readers' theater treatment of, 147–48,
149–51; Tlingit and Tagish legend
compared to experiences of, 7
written sources, emphasis on, 3

Y

Yellow Woman and a Beauty of the Spirit
(Silko), 117
youth: artwork of, *110;* learning stories,
challenges to, 31; work with, 12,
100, 110–11
Yukon College, 7
Yup'ik Eskimo: ceremonies of, 26;
clothing of, 37–38, 52, 54, 56,
57, 58, 71–72 (*see also* parka as